A SYMPHONY OF FROGS
An Autobiography

BY MARY (TROYER) BERGEY
WITH LEROY MILLER

Cover art by Kathy Bergey Silsley

THE
DONNING COMPANY
PUBLISHERS

Copyright © 1997 by Mary Bergey

All rights reserved, including the right to reproduce this work in any form whatsoever without permission in writing from the publisher, except for brief passages in connection with a review.

For information, write:
THE DONNING COMPANY/PUBLISHERS
184 Business Park drive, Suite 106
Virginia Beach, VA 23462

Steve Mull, *General Manager*
B. L. Walton Jr., *Project Director*
Dawn V. Kofroth, Assistant *General Manager*
Richard A. Horwege, *Senior Editor*
Misty Taylor, *Graphic Designer*
Teri S. Arnold, *Senior Marketing Coordinator*

Library of Congress Cataloging-in-Publication Data
Bergey, Mary Troyer, 1928-
A symphony of frogs : an autobiography / by Mary (Troyer) Bergey ; with Leroy Miller.
    p.   cm.
    Includes index.
    ISBN 1-57864-016-4 (hardcover : alk. paper)
    ISBN 1-57864-018-0 (pbk. : alk. paper)
    1. Bergey, Mary Troyer, 1928–   . 2. Mennonites–United States–Biography. 3. Missionaries–Albania–Biography. 4. Missionaries–United States–Biography.   I. Miller, Leroy, 1937–   II. Title.
BX8143.B45A3   1997
289.7'092-dc21
[B]   97-35965
                                                                    CIP

Printed in the United States of America

Table of Contents

Preface 1

Chapter 1.
Midnight Girl 3

Chapter 2.
Roots 13

Chapter 3.
Off Puddin' Ridge 21

Chapter 4.
To Market, to Market 31

Chapter 5.
The Rising Tide 39

Chapter 6.
Tears by Turns 49

Chapter 7.
Soul Guardians 57

Chapter 8.
Love's Promise 63

Chapter 9.
The Commitment 71

Chapter 10.
A New Direction 79

Chapter 11.
Your People Shall Be My People 89

Chapter 12.
As Long As We Both Shall Live 97

Chapter 13.
Joy and Heartbreak 105

Chapter 14.
Pursuing the Goal 115

Chapter 15.
The Music Plays On 129

Index 138

PREFACE

WHEN Leroy Miller first suggested in early 1993, that I should consider doing an autobiography, the prospect of a published work seemed an unlikely dream. But with God's direction and much persistence, "the book" has finally become a reality. The telling of one's life story is not an easy undertaking. Coupled with the constraints of time are the mental and emotional difficulties involved. Accurately recalling dates and details after fifty-plus years is sometimes all but impossible. Then, there is also the problem of calling forth incidents from the past. To relive a half-forgotten sorrow or other hurtful episode may stir memories that were better left buried. Beyond that lies the vulnerability factor. Openly sharing your innermost feelings can leave one exposed to criticism and second-guessing from total strangers.

Yet, in spite of the drawbacks, this endeavor has turned into a most rewarding experience. Through the many hours of written notes and interviews, I have reached a far better understanding of myself and those influences, and persons as well, that have molded me into who I am today.

Mary and James Bergey in 1983.

While I trust many persons will be blessed by what is contained here, I specifically wish to dedicate my story to our grandchildren, as an expression of James' and my heartfelt love for them. May the book's message encourage young people everywhere, to consider the importance of decisions made during their teens and early twenties. Certainly, the Christian life does not spare us from deep disappointments, personal grief and financial worries; nevertheless, coming from one who has "been there," I can firmly attest, the choice to follow God's will brings immeasurable joy and a peace that is beyond understanding.

"*Thou wilt shew me the path of life: in thy presence is fullness of joy; at thy right hand there are pleasures for evermore.*"
(Psalm 16:11) King James Version.

Mary Bergey
May 1997

Chapter 1
Midnight Girl

The fields along Cooper-Garret Road stretch away in the distance, the soybeans, dark green and healthy in the overcast August afternoon. "Stop here," I tell husband James. "I'm sure the place was right along here."

My eyes search for something that will mark the spot I'm hoping to locate. But in vain, there is nothing. No tree, shrub or dilapidated building to indicate the land has ever produced anything more than field crops. A pang of sadness strikes as I contemplate the utter disappearance of everything that was once so much of my childhood.

"See, there," James speaks beside me. "Where the beans are slightly off-color? That usually indicates where buildings once stood. I believe the yellowish tint comes from boron left in the soil."

Thanks to a lifetime of farming, my husband's trained eye has found the former site of my parents' farmstead, here in Currituck County, North Carolina. Scant though the trace, it is enough to sharpen the images recently flickering across my memory.

* * *

Grandma Malinda Miller stood at the edge of her garden, leaning on the hoe handle, her head slightly bowed. Dear, sweet Grandma! While planting or weeding, she occasionally stopped to pray for God's bounty from the ground. Raising her head, she beckoned. Delightedly, I scampered across the yard to meet her. Grandma dug into her apron pocket, searching for the treat she always kept there, store-bought corn candy. "Here, Mary, I have something for you," she said, hand extended.

The orange and yellow kernels dropped into my open palm. I murmured a quick "Thanks," before sinking my teeth into the sweet, chewy goodness. In that moment, an insistent calling interrupted the pleasant moment. "Mary! Mary! Come, get up! It's

Grandma Malinda (Slabaugh) Miller, circa 1950.

time to help Mom with breakfast."

Dad's voice had broken into my dream, and Grandma disappeared in the waking reality of our upstairs bedroom. Already out of bed and getting dressed, sister Fannie clomped about the carpetless floor in her workday shoes. The kerosene lamp's orange light cast her movements in vague, jerky shadows against the painted white walls and ceiling. Outlined in the dim glow, were the room's sparse furnishings–three double beds, a mirrorless dresser and small nightstand.

At that moment, I could not have cared less about the noise Fannie made, or what furniture might be lacking. The cozy warmth under the heavy comforter and quilt begged me to snuggle down into dreams that included my Grandma. Breakfast, work, school–none seemed exciting this cold winter morning.

Fully dressed, Fannie made certain I would not fall asleep again. "Come on, Mary. Right now! I'll pull the covers off, if you don't get up."

Grabbing a corner of the comforter, she pulled while I clutched the covers around me. Fannie, three years older, easily won the tug-of-war with her superior strength. With the covers down, I jumped out of bed and dashed to the chamber pot. Oooh, the metal graniteware was cold against my skin, though not half so bad as running to the outdoor privy in the backyard.

As on any other morning, I wasted no time deciding what to wear—the blue one was clean for today. I had three school dresses, solid colors of green, purplish-lavender, and blue. All were identically made, collarless, small buttons in front, with skirt and waist sewn together. The dresses, in fact, all our clothes were homemade, cut out by Mom or an older sister and sewed on the treadle sewing machine.

I slipped into the dress and pulled on thick black *shtrimp*, stripping flat elastic garters over my knees to hold the stockings in place. No decent Amish girl or woman would have dared go out in public without wearing these long heavy cotton stockings. They were warm in cold weather, but hot and sticky otherwise. Running in them was most difficult, and one had but two choices. You either hunched forward, desperately grabbing at your knees and slowing your progress, or you ran straight up while the stocking crawled down around your ankles. During summer, I often wished to be rid of them, Sometimes, attempting to be fashionable like other girls who wore ankle socks, I would roll the stocking down to my shoe tops. The result, I'm sure, was far less stylish than I thought it to be.

Once dressed, I made sure little brother Bud was awake, then hurried downstairs. Brewed coffee, fried pork and scrambled eggs—the good smells greeted me when I opened the door into the darkened living room. The kitchen's pleasant warmth was a delightful contrast to the frigid bedroom that I had just left.

"Good morning, Mary," Mom, stirring a kettle on the cookstove, greeted me with a smile. "Wash up. Then you can set the table. Breakfast is almost ready, and Dad and the girls will soon be done choring."

A peek into the kettle and frying pan revealed a couple of my favorites: tomato gravy and pork brains with scrambled eggs.

Yummy. There was no time to dawdle, though. Filling the washbasin with several strokes on the pitcher pump, I cupped my hands to splash water on my face and scrubbed vigorously to wash the last bit of sleep from my eyes.

I set the plates, coffee mugs, and silverware at their proper places on the oilcloth tablecover. Dad at the head of the table, Mom on the corner, then sisters, Edna and Fannie, with Bud and me on the bench along the back. Dad and the girls came in, and Mom began dishing up the food. I put the milk pitcher, butter and jelly dishes on the table. "Edna if you slice the bread, we'll be ready to eat," Mom said.

With everyone seated, we bowed our heads as Dad asked the blessing–the same German prayer he always recited before we ate. Breakfast was typical of our meals: the clink of spoons against plates and the sounds of chewing. Unlike some families where lively chatter and food go together, we were expected to be quiet around the table. Dad considered mealtime conversation unnecessary noise. Sometimes, he kept a switch by his chair to enforce the rules. When one of us displayed what he saw as poor behavior–slouching or dawdling over our food–the switch flicked out to catch the offender on the head or shoulder. Also, no one left

Uncle Jonas Miller with Bud and me in 1931.

the table until everyone had finished eating, after which we again bowed our heads, while Dad returned thanks for God's provisions.

"Mary, you and Bud will have to hurry," Mom said, getting up from the table. "The weather is bad this morning, so it will take longer to get to the bus stop."

Mom had our lunches packed, bologna between two slices of home-baked bread and an apple in each bag. Even our lunches made us different from the other schoolchildren. Nearly everyone else carried biscuits and molasses in metal lunchboxes, while we had brown paper bags that had to be folded and reused as long as they would last.

"Put on your heavy coats and boots, children," Mom ordered. "It's cloudy and the north wind is sharp this morning."

"Oh, goody, maybe it will snow," I said, excitedly. "I hope it snows so deep we can't go to school for a whole week. Don't you hope so too, Bud? We'll make a big snowman."

My blonde, chubby-faced brother grinned, the usual response to his talkative older sister.

"Well, Mary, maybe it will snow," Mom said. "It doesn't seem quite cold enough yet, but it's colder than yesterday."

That was Mom, and I loved her for it. Offering hope and encouragement, sometimes even when there wasn't much for which to hope. Snow was a rarity here in northeast North Carolina, and seldom accumulated to more than an inch or two. We pulled on boots and coats, and I tied my black *kupduch* (bandanna) under my chin. Bud had his *tsippelkop* (stocking cap) down on the sides to cover his ears. Mom tugged his coat around him and buttoned the top button. "Yes, so you'll stay warm," Mom insisted to Bud's squirming and protests. "It's not choking you."

"Bye, Mom," I called, opening the kitchen door.

"Goodbye, children," Mom replied. "*Mary, nau geb gut acht uff der Bud*" (Take good care of Bud).

"*Yah.*" She need not remind me. I always looked after my little brother. Bud was only two years younger than I, but I had learned early to be responsible for him. Mom and my older sisters, Malinda and Lizzie, had seen to that.

* * * *

Roads, like almost everything else on earth, usually change over time. They are widened, paved, and straightened; however, after six decades the changes to our old road are minor. The dead end is gone, since being tied into a connecting road. The official Cooper-Garret title gives the road a touch of class, lacking in our "Chitlin' Switch" and "Pigtail Avenue" nicknames. The roadbed is still unpaved, though in much better condition than when we and our neighbors traveled over it every day.

During winter and rainy weather the road became a slash of black mud, laced with water-filled ruts left by buggy and truck wheels. In that condition, the mile walk to the school bus stop at Puddin' Ridge Road turned into a hard trek for Bud and me. We picked our way carefully, trying to avoid the worst places. It seemed to take forever to get to the first bridge, only a quarter mile from home. Beyond that was the Coopers' place. The one consolation on cold days was that Mrs. Cooper stayed in her warm kitchen. Bud and I were afraid of her, for she was often unhappy and spoke crossly when she saw us children.

Although I never relished the walk, Bud and I made a game of it during pleasant weather. We marked our progress by trees that were like old friends–tulip poplar, a couple huge oaks, and bald cypress. Sometimes wild rabbits hopped along the way; bobwhites called across the open fields; and the rich, heady perfume of wild honeysuckle filled the air. Best of all, for me, the most intriguing spots along the road were two big drainage canals.

The watercourses were home to a vast horde of frogs, and summer nights brought on a million-voice choir. Small peepers melded their rapid high-pitched trill with the mid-range "yennng" of their larger cousins, while the big bullfrogs' "kachung" added an off-beat bass rhythm. On wind-still evenings the tuneless clamor could be heard from a great distance. I never tired of this tumult that often lulled me to sleep, embedding itself into my childhood memories in a manner I would not begin to understand until long afterward.

The worst part of the long walk involved my anxiety over our arrival at the bus stop. We never quite knew what reception awaited us from the "English" kids–all non-Amish were English to us. Usually, they left us alone; however, sometimes the taunts would begin before we reached Puddin Ridge. "Midnight! Midnight! Here comes the Midnights!"

Even on cold days, the words brought a hot rush of shame. We knew we were different, but why did they need to remind us with that ugly chant? Though we were Old Order Amish, community people knew us as Mennonites, and "Midnight" had become our nickname in the public schools. The derogatory label did nothing for my already low self-esteem, but merely reinforced my childhood belief, that we Amish could expect little else from a hard, uncaring world.

* * * *

"Boys and girls, please, pay attention," Mrs. Smith tapped her chalk against the blackboard. "Understanding fractions is an important part of arithmetic. Imagine, this circle is a large pie. When we cut it across once, each part is one-half. If we slice the halves in two, each part is one-fourth. Let's divide those again to make eighths. Now, who can tell me, how many eighths make one-half?"

Please, don't call on me, I begged silently. Being asked to answer in class was dreadful enough, when I was sure of the answer. Arithmetic was my worst subject, and fractions were the hardest part. Suddenly, I felt Mrs. Smith's gaze fix on me. "Mary, can you tell the class how many eighths are in one-half?"

Swallowing hard, I hesitantly answered, "Is it four?"

"That is correct," Mrs. Smith beamed. "Very good, Mary."

My face felt hot with embarrassment. Why did Teacher have to say that? I knew the whole class was staring at me, and I wished to run away and hide. Instead, I sat with eyes downcast until the uncomfortable moment passed. The 100 grade on a spelling test later that day was much easier to handle. No one besides Mrs. Smith knew about that.

The village school at Moyock, North Carolina, was an intimidating place for all the six-and-one-half years I attended there. Though it could not begin to match the size and sleek lines of modern school buildings, the large-windowed brick two-story building had classrooms for grades one through eleven. If the size and number of so many strange people were not scary enough, I had the added problem of speaking almost no English when I entered first grade in 1934. In our rural isolation, we children had heard little else but our native Pennsylvania German before starting school.

So far as I can recall, none of my teachers at Moyock ever treated me unkindly because of our cultural and religious difference. Sister Fannie, in fact, remembers at least one or more of her teachers made a special effort to help her feel accepted. I have also since concluded some of the students' insults, we believed came from our being Amish, were merely part of the misbehavior that goes on at most schools. Standing out from the crowd can make one an easy target for abuse; however, past generations of Amish and Mennonite children learned early about their persecution heritage. As a result, it became easy to don our martyrs' cloaks at the first shove or crude remark.

One of my most frightening experiences at Moyock school occurred on my way to the second-floor classrooms. Someone bumped me from behind as I was starting up the stairs. When I turned, Billy, a big boy, confronted me, holding a knife with the blade out. "Girl, see this?" he said, scowling. "I'm gonna cut yo' head off."

Although, I now believe Billy only intended to scare me, at the time I was sure my life was in grave danger. Heart racing madly, I dashed up the stairs and down the hall to my classroom. Not until

I was safely inside did I dare glance over my shoulder to make certain Billy wasn't at my heels. Sliding into my seat, I covered my fright as best I could, not wishing to answer questions about why I was breathing so hard.

Only on the playing field did I come close to feeling at ease and accepted. Being able to hit and catch a baseball raised my self-confidence like nothing else. For reasons I can't explain, a teammate's "Yay, Mary," and "Good catch, girl," did not trigger the impulse to duck and turn away, as when a teacher paid me a compliment.

While timidity all but controlled my school hours, the one exception was anything that threatened little brother Bud's well-being. The moment anyone encroached there. my protective instincts took over. I would rush to his aid without hesitation. The worst times were after school, while waiting for our bus. Everyone wanted to be as close to the head of the line as possible, since those first on the bus had their choice of seats. Together, Bud and I were okay, but the trouble came when he was in line several places to the rear. Older boys would then sometimes pester and shove Bud out of his place in line.

Dropping my books on the sidewalk, I was like a mother hen defending its chick, no matter the cost. I would go at the bully—sometimes two—with fists flying. The tactic usually worked. The tormenters would back off; maybe, surprised by my audacity, or not wanting to be charged with fighting a girl.

Those episodes left me shaken and empty, wanting to be quiet and left alone on the bus ride back to Puddin' Ridge. However, I wasn't always so fortunate. I remember once when Jack, a sixth-grader began badgering me with questions I thought were too shameful to answer: "How do Midnights date? Do they hug and kiss?"

Goodness! What kind of persons did he think we were?

* * * *

Going in Chitlin' Switch always seemed shorter than the

walk out to the bus stop. The reason may have been because I loved my home so dearly, especially this afternoon. Sight of the house in the distance helped me forget some of the day's unhappy moments. In my mind's eye, I could already see the living room scene the moment we opened the front door. Mom would be at the sewing machine, feet busily tramping the treadle, while her practiced hands guided the material into the rapidly moving needle. The finished piece might be new denim pants for Bud, or an everyday dress for me, made from cotton feed bag cloth, dyed light blue or green. Dad in his rocking chair, reading *The Pathfinder* or *Grit*, would look up and nod. Anticipation quickened my steps before Bud's plaintive wail broke my daydream. "Wait, Mary. Wait for me. You're going too fast."

Slowing, I turned and called, "Hurry up, and I'll tell you something good."

"You're just saying that," he said, breaking into a shuffling half-trot. "Will I like it?"

"Yes, you will," I assured, allowing him to catch up. "After we get home, I'll ask Dad to give us some of his Emulsion."

Bud's grin told me I hadn't deceived him. When Dad was in a good mood, and I used my best pleading tone, he would sometimes get out of his chair, go to his desk, bring out the bottle of cold medicine and give us each a sample. We never got more than a teaspoonful of Emulsion, but brother and I savored those moments as special. We loved the anise-licorice flavor, and I believe knowing we were getting a taste of grownup medicine made it all the more delicious.

I'll race you," Bud called over his shoulder, now already a half-dozen steps ahead. While I could have easily outrun his short stubby legs, I let him hold the lead, as we dashed through the mud toward home.

Chapter 2
Roots

MY DAD, John S. Troyer, was what has sometimes been called "mechanically inclined." Had he been born in another time and place, John might have gone on to fully develop his natural abilities. An engineering degree from Ohio State University might have given him entrance into research and development with a major auto or farm equipment manufacturer. Such opportunities, however, were rare even in the best of circumstances during the early 1900s, and impossible for an Old Order Amish boy who expected to stay with the church.

Going to college would have been preposterous, for John, the oldest of Simon Troyer's ten children. At the beginning of the twentieth century, few Amish children received more than minimal schooling: enough math to do sums, along with elementary reading and writing skills. According to Amish thought, nothing more was necessary–boys were destined to be farmers and girls were meant to be farmers' wives.

A young man with a bent for something other than tilling the soil and keeping farm animals could turn to blacksmithing, carpentry, milling, or a related vocation. Hard work is man's lot here on earth. God had commanded it when He drove Adam and Eve from Eden. "In the sweat of thy face shalt thou eat bread. . . ." To think anything else was out of the question.

Born July 20, 1892, John Troyer spent his early years near Elkhart, Indiana. His mother, Mary, died when he was eight. A year later, he and his seven-year-old sister, Elizabeth, moved with their father to Ohio, when their father married Barbara Miller. John grew to manhood in the area of Charm village, in Holmes County. Along with learning farming methods of that day, he also developed carpentry and other woodworking skills. John's greatest interest, however, seems to have been in machinery. He bought a threshing machine after turning twenty-one in 1913, and with a

My father, John S. Troyer, was a good farmer. Here he is in his cornfield, circa 1960.

crew of helpers went about the countryside threshing grain for farmers. Later, he owned a successful planing mill.

Around 1915–16, John traveled to the Amish community at Exelund, in Sawyer County, Wisconsin. There, the young Lincolnesque six-footer found himself smitten by teenager Dena Miller. Almost petite, the blue-eyed brunette could have set any youthful suitor's heart fluttering. A smooth, clear complexion gave Dena "a pretty woman" label that would follow her into middle-age. If the cliché that "opposites attract" is ever true, it certainly was for this pair. Rudy Miller's third child and oldest daughter's sunny disposition and warm friendliness contrasted sharply against John's personality. He was quiet and moody with a smoldering temper that sometimes flared out of control.

Precisely how long John remained at Exelund is unknown. However, he and Dena carried on a courtship by mail after he returned home to Ohio. In fact, his marriage proposal and her acceptance were accomplished through letters. Late in 1916, or shortly after New Year 1917, John, then twenty-four, returned to Wisconsin, and the two were married February 4, 1917–five weeks before Dena's seventeenth birthday.

Over the next few years, my parents moved twice from Exelund back to Ohio. My oldest brother, Alvin, was born in Holmes County, January 1, 1918. Sixteen months later, Mom gave birth to their second child, Malinda, at Exelund. By September 1920, when Lizzie came along, John Troyers were back in Holmes County. Though, they would eventually move again, three more children were born in Ohio: Edna, Fannie, and a son who died in infancy. Afterward, Dena often recalled details about baby John's death, and how close she herself came to dying in childbirth.

Rootlessness–characteristic of the United States' mobile generation in the 1990s–is nothing new for the Amish. Throughout their 300-year history, they have been a people on the move. First, in Europe, religious persecution drove them from one country to another in search of a safe haven. Later, here in America, the promise of cheap land lured succeeding generations of Amish families to the far horizon. The new home might not be Eden, but hopefully, it would be better than the weather-plagued, hilly, dry, stony place they were leaving behind.

Grandpa Rudy Miller may not have set a record among those seekers after a Promised Land, but he must have come close. A native Kansan, Rudy married Malinda Slaubaugh at Mylo, North Dakota. In sixty years of marriage, they lived twice in Montana, once each in Wisconsin, Ohio, North Carolina, Virginia, and finally, in Indiana. Six children grew to adulthood, but during this long trek, dear Grandma had eleven more babies who died in infancy.

Except for the one move to Wisconsin, Mom and Dad lived

Grandpa Rudy Miller smoking a pipe, circa 1950.

in the Holmes and Wayne Counties' area during their early years of marriage. By 1927, my parents should have been content to raise their family in Ohio. Dad owned a lumber planing mill near Fredricksburg. The older children were attending the one-room Leeper's School, a mile from home. Life, however, was not as serene as it appeared. Seven years earlier a new force had been added to the ingrained Amish migration urge. The Ohio General Assembly had passed a rigid school attendance law in 1921. Known as the Bing Act, the law required that all children must attend a certified school until age eighteen; though in certain cases a work permit could be obtained at age sixteen. The new law caused widespread dismay among the Amish. Those who refused to comply soon felt the iron fist of state government. A number of Old Order Amish fathers were arrested and jailed, others paid fines. Several families had their children taken away after the state declared them wards of the court. The children were placed in a children's home, where they were forced to wear "English" clothes.

This and the fear of further persecution stirred several Amish families to move to Mexico. Grandpa Simon Troyers were among those who left the United States in 1922. Dad's younger half brothers and half sister were still school age at the time. Since my siblings were too young then for the Bing Act to be a personal threat, my parents felt no pressure to follow Grandpa Troyers.

A year or two later, though, Dad began having health problems. He contracted pneumonia during the winter two or three years following. His doctor told him, "Mister Troyer, for your health's sake, you must find a warmer climate, away from this Ohio cold."

Mom and Dad began looking southward, but not to Mexico. That settlement was not prospering, and there were growing signs it wouldn't last many more years.

About the time Mom and Dad were married, a small Old Order community had sprung up on the eastern edge of North Carolina's Dismal Swamp. Two land agents, John Selp and Ed Schilders, from Chillicothe, Ohio, solicited Amish farmers to develop the reclaimed swampland. John Selp was especially aggressive with his promotion. Besides having two large drainage canals dug across his tract, he offered living space in his big roomy hotel for arriving settlers, until they had built their own houses and barns. The hotel had been built originally to house loggers working in the swamp.

The Moyock settlement grew slowly during the 1920s. However, along with Selp's and Schilders' personal contacts with Amish prospects, the Sugarcreek, Ohio, *Budget* carried newsletters from the North Carolina settlement. The writers gave glowing reports of productive farmland, mild climate, good markets, as well as other area advantages. Sometime in 1927, John Troyer became convinced it was time to leave Ohio. He told his wife and children, "We're moving to North Carolina."

The planing mill at Fredricksburg was sold. Household furniture and whatever else had not been sold at auction, including tools and two big workhorses, were loaded onto a railroad car—the horses died within the year, unable to stand the southern heat and humidity. Shortly after New Year 1928, John Troyer, his seven-months pregnant wife and five children, ages three through ten, boarded a passenger train for the trip south. Judged against even the family's own spartan living standards, the two-day journey was no excursion. The poorly heated coaches' loose windows leaked winter air and coal smoke from the steam locomotive. Greasy soot smeared everything it touched—clothes, hands, and faces. The Troyers, tired and grimy, resembled a coal mine crew when they finally climbed off the train at Norfolk, Virginia.

They spent overnight with the John B. Yoder family at Beech Grove, near Kempsville, Virginia, before traveling the last twenty-five miles to Moyock, just south of the Virginia–North Carolina line. On their arrival at Moyock, the family moved into the back part of John Selp's hotel along Puddin' Ridge Road. Amish church services were held in the front section of the building.

Only by a stretch of the imagination, could the structure have been considered a hotel. True, it had a long hall down the center with rooms on each side. But the place had no electricity or any semblance of indoor plumbing. As a child in later years, I remember the building as a great play area after Sunday services. We children chased one another down the long hall and back, squealing with laughter as we ran through the empty rooms.

Barely two months after arriving in the new community, Mom was admitted to Saint Vincent's Hospital in Norfolk. I was born there March 6, 1928. A hospital birth for an Amish child was most unusual for the 1920s. Nearly all deliveries occurred at home, and at this late date no one quite knows why Mom went to the hospital for her seventh child. Sister Edna believes it may have been because of the baby who died between Fannie and me. Mom used to say, "The doctor killed that baby."

Mom repeated the story of my birth, until I knew it by heart. How I had been born with a perfect veil—actually the amniotic membrane—over my face. Because of its rare occurrence, past folklore held that good fortune comes to the child so born. One of the Catholic nuns told Mom, "Yes, indeed, Mrs. Troyer, the veil promises good things. This child is special!"

Mom was impressed enough with the nun Mary Jane's pronouncement to name me after her. I am the only one in our family with a middle name—adding a middle name was considered a mark of pride among the Amish in times past. As a young girl, I sometimes thought about the unique role in which the veil had, supposedly, placed me. I tried my best to do things that would show others I was a good person. However, growing older, I realized no physical feature at birth, nor doing good deeds later could make me righteous in God's sight. That can come only by my being His workmanship in Jesus Christ.

According to my sister Edna, I was privileged with another first in our family. Back in Ohio, Mom and Dad were members of the Sam Yoder Church. The Sam Yoders had the strictest rules of any Old Order Amish district. Mothers there were required to wear black flannel diapers on their babies. The church at Moyock made no attempt to regulate babies' underwear, and Mom cheered at the freedom to put me in white cotton diapers.

While she gained some unaccustomed liberty in that instance, that was not always true. Having grown up out West—where church rules were not always as strictly enforced as here in the East—Mom's less than total commitment to Amish tradition sometimes left her at odds with Dad's side of the family and other members of the church.

Chapter 3
Off Puddin' Ridge

My early childhood memories are mostly pleasant. I loved our place off Puddin' Ridge, and felt secure there during my first ten years. In the year we had lived at Selp's hotel, Dad had built the house and barn with some help from the men of the Amish community. Later, outbuildings included a butcher house, chicken house, and summer kitchen.

We did our canning in the summer kitchen, and also ate there during the warm months. The masonry block and wood-sided building had an A roof and stood a short distance from the house. A scary incident happened there for me, when I was about five or six. My place was on the wooden bench along back of the table at mealtime. I fell asleep one evening after supper, sprawled on the bench and out of sight. No one apparently noticed I wasn't around to help dry dishes. Twilight came and everyone else, tired from a summer day's work, went to the house and bed. Much later, I awakened in thick darkness. Panicked, I felt my way outside, across the wet grass to the back porch. Twisting and turning the knob desperately, I couldn't budge the door. *"Mem! Mem!"* I called loudly between sobs. After what seemed forever to a small child, Mom came to unlock the door and let me in. She soothed me and soon I was upstairs, snuggled in bed with sister Fannie, where I belonged.

The farmhouse, a white clapboard two-story, faced the road; its straight, simple lines showing the influence of plain Midwest Amish design. A roofed front porch, supported by wooden posts, ran the full length of the house. Downstairs were a large living room, Mom and Dad's bedroom, a pantry, and the kitchen with a back door that opened onto a screen-enclosed stoop. Two upstairs bedrooms belonged to us children, the smaller room for Alvin and Bud, and the larger one for my sisters and me.

I remember one place in the house I did not like–the closet under the stairs. While Mom banished me there only a time or two,

The house my father built in 1928, the year I was born.

older sister Malinda was far less lenient. Nine years older than I, Malinda mothered us younger children, while Mom attended market in Norfolk. Depending upon Malinda's mood, it didn't take a major infraction for her to stick little Mary into that close, dark cell. The punishment left me terror-stricken. With no electricity, there was no light to snap on in the tight cubicle. I would sit and sob quietly, surrounded by darkness, thinking I might die before the door opened again. Would they weep and feel sorry I wondered, if they found me with eyes closed and no longer breathing.

The house had no bathtub or commode, hot or cold water from a faucet and most of the things we consider absolute necessities today. Nevertheless, it seemed comfortable enough at the time. Looking back, I do not believe I gave much thought to the things we might have lacked. I had learned, quite young, the importance of not being worldly, as were all non-Amish persons. Doing without modern conveniences kept us from worldliness.

As a little girl, I was full of idealism. Home and family were my greatest treasures. My heart welled with joy to hear Mom laugh or singing in her strong, throaty voice, while she went about her work. I loved to join in when she sang something familiar. Her songs ranged from folk ballads, such as "Barbara Allen," to slow German church hymns. It didn't matter that I couldn't always follow the words. Mom singing, meant she was happy, and that always pleased me.

Here I am, at left, by our house with my sisters Lizzie (holding the dog), Edna, and Fannie.

Like many Amish families from the Midwest, laughter—sometimes loud, unrestrained hooting—was an active part of our household. Small things, a mispronounced word, pratfall, or the antics of a farm animal became sources of humor for later recall to be laughed over again.

Mom taught us Pennsylvania German ditties and nursery rhymes, two of which I remember in particular. The first is an adult's chant to a tot being bounced on a knee, where at the end the child is tilted sideways, as though being thrown from the horse. We small ones delighted in this game over and over, until the bouncer gave up in exhaustion.

> *Reide, reide geili,*
> *Der becker shlacht en seili,*
> *Der miller shlacht en rote kuh,*
> *Mutter, darf ich aw die tsu?*
> *Nay, 'siss en gar base kuh.*
> (Ride a, ride a horsey,
> The baker slaughters a little sow,
> The miller slaughters a red cow,
> Mother, may I be there too?
> No, 'tis a very angry cow.)

Another favorite was the lullaby:
> *Shloff, bubbly, shloff,*
> *Der Dawdy hiet de Shoff.*

Die Mummy hiet de kieh,
Sie bahd in der dreck
Bis an die gnie,
Und kummt net heem
Bis marye frie,
Shloff, bubbly, shloff.
(Sleep, baby, sleep,
Daddy herds the sheep.
Mother herds the cows,
And wades in muck up to her knees,
And won't be home 'til tomorrow morning.)

Evenings, we'd gather in the living room and Dad would read from the Bible, after which we knelt and he read a long prayer from the German prayer book. I understood next to nothing of the High German text; nevertheless, those times together left me with a child's sense of God's nearness, and a warmth for my parents and siblings.

There are many other good memories of that time. Mom's brother Andy's family lived near us, and Bud and I often played with our cousins, Ilo and Marietta. Though we had no store-bought toys, our fun came from simple games and imagination. We played, "Ain't No Bears Out Tonight,"–frighteningly scary in the darkness– "Tag," and "Ring Around the Roses." We rode broomstick horses with string bridles and made mud pies. Mud pie making held special excitement on the few occasions we managed to sneak a fresh egg or two from the henhouse to mix with the pretend pastry. Getting caught meant certain banishment to the stair closet!

For a time, Grandma Malinda and Grandpa Rudy Miller lived about a mile from our place. They had arrived from Bloomfield, Montana, in 1930, before I can remember. I always enjoyed the walk to Grandma's house, where visits often included a big, delicious sugar cookie or the yellow corn candy she kept on hand. Those were unforgettable times for me.

Although, I was drawn to Grandma by the strength of her

Left to right, back row: sister Malinda, friend Madge, sister Edna, sister Lizzie, brother Alvin, and neighbor Harvey Sullivan. Front row: Esther Sullivan, Marie McAmore holding Eddie Sullivan, Uncle Jonas Miller holding Bud and me, and sister Fannie.

warm, gentle spirit, I did not feel much attachment to Grandpa Rudy. He was very strict, insisting that Grandma obey the Amish traditions, as he understood them to be. It seemed to me, Rudy sometimes treated Grandma unkindly. When I was six, Grandpa decided to pull up stakes again. They moved this time to Deep Creek, Virginia, about twenty miles away, but still too far for me to see Grandma very often. Long ago though it's been, the sadness and sense of loss I felt over their leaving are still vivid memories today. Grandpa Millers lived last at Nappanee, Indiana, where husband, James, and I visited them after we were married, several years before Grandma's death in 1956.

After Uncle Andy's family, the Coopers were our nearest neighbors. They and their daughter, Donna Faye, lived beyond the first canal. Donna Faye was about my older sisters' age, and sometimes attended the Amish youngfolks' Sunday evening singings with them. Bud and I never spent much time at the Coopers. While we were rather fond of Mister Cooper, a good-natured, pipe-smoking gentleman, we tried our best to avoid Mrs. Cooper. A heavy-set woman, who seldom smiled, Mrs. Cooper would speak her mind about anything that displeased her. In summertime, she fussed about the dust our vehicles stirred going by their place. Ruts left by our wagon and buggy wheels gave her more reason to complain during wet spells.

We also had a black neighbor family for several years. The lady, known as Aunt Mandy, lived with a widower and his two children. The boy, Andrew, and his sister–Sara, if I recall correctly–were about the age of Bud and me. We often played with them and walked to the school bus stop together. Of course, back then, we rode the bus for whites and they rode a separate bus to their own "colored" school. This was long before whites could have dreamed integrated schools as being possible.

Among all the enjoyable social times of visiting and play, few were more delightful than those occasions when several of the Amish young people came to our house to sing and play guitar with my older sisters. Listening to the Overholt twins' beautiful harmony gave me goose bumps. John and Joe played and sang in the musical style of the Delmore Brothers, a popular Nashville recording duo at that time.

Though too young to participate, I hung close at every opportunity, watching the finger movements to learn how the various chords were formed. Sometimes, when I was supposed to be in bed, I would creep to the head of the stairs, the better to absorb the wonderful sound coming from the living room below. Next day, I would sit down with Edna or Fannie's guitar and practice over and over, trying to coax those same mellow tones from the strings.

The struggle was worth the effort. For more than half a century, my guitar has been a cherished possession. Although, I laid it aside for a number of years–our former bishop, Eli Kramer, sharply opposed musical instruments, even at home–playing guitar has brought me much pleasure. It's lifted my low spirits and given voice to joy for which I might not otherwise have found expression. More than that, I trust others have been blessed by the message that comes through the hymns and Gospel songs.

For all the enjoyable memories of early home life at Moyock,

Left to right: John Overholt with guitar, sister Edna, brother Alvin, Delilah Overholt, sister Malinda, sister Lizzie, John Miller in back, and Joseph Overholt with violin. Abner Overholt is in front with banjo.

there were enough unpleasant incidents to make life less than idyllic. About age ten, I spent several weeks in bed with a fever and a circular area of painful rash on my back. When the illness refused to yield to Mom's store of home remedies, she summoned the doctor-in those days, doctors made house calls to places even as remote as ours. "This child has shingles," the doctor informed Mom, knowingly.

He prescribed treatment and left ointment, neither of which had any effect on my ailment. Finally, in desperation, Mom took me to Deep Creek, Virginia, to a *braucher*–a word probably from the German, "practice" or "custom." This man had a reputation for healing difficult medical problems. Seating me on a chair in the middle of the living room, the *braucher* gathered several burning embers from the stove onto a small metal shovel. He then began a strange, unintelligible chant, all the while walking circles around me, until he had completed ten or more rounds. By then, the glowing coals had cooled, turned black, and the treatment ended. Bizarre as the episode was, within a day or two afterward, I had recovered from my sickness.

While the eerie ritual seems to have brought about a cure, I have since renounced the experience. I believe *brauching* is an evil, occult practice, left over from northern Europe's ancient pagan culture. True believers in Jesus should recognize *brauching* for what it is: a form of witchcraft! In fact this particular braucher's nickname, "The Devil's Walking Stick," proves the point.

Some things that seemed dreadful at the time resulted more from our isolated location, rather than the reality. The road ended about a mile beyond our place, so there was no through traffic. An approaching motor vehicle would send me and Bud scampering, wide-eyed with fright and calling, *Mem! Mem! Ebbah kummt!*" ("Mom! Mom! Someone's coming!").

The intruder usually turned out to be the delivery truck bringing hog or chicken feed. During warm weather, the iceman brought big blocks of ice for the house and butcher house iceboxes. The Raleigh man drove in less frequently with his wares–boxes of herbs and spices, bottles and metal tins of all sizes, that contained everything from vanilla extract to elixirs, liniments and salves, touted to be "Good for Man or Beast."

This store on wheels was an important service to us and other country dwellers. Remember, there were no supermarkets at the time. We bought our staples, such as flour, sugar, and salt at Creekmore's General Store in Moyock. The nearest drugstore was in Portsmouth or Norfolk, twenty or more miles away. However, that did not really matter, since in serious medical cases doctors dispensed their own medicines, rather than writing a prescription as is done today.

While much of our childish fear of strangers was unfounded, there was one person in our area of whom even some grownups were wary. Riley Powers, a fellow in his twenties, lived in a shack near the end of our road. He hauled his meager supplies in a rickety pushcart and would come by our place, singing and talking loudly to no one in particular.

Riley sometimes stopped at our house to talk with Dad. On

one such occasion, I had a terrifying encounter with him. Coming home from school one afternoon, I opened the front door to find Dad and Riley talking in the living room. For no apparent reason, Riley picked up the stove poker, opened the pot-bellied stove and speared a live coal. Turning, he grinned wickedly and came at me with the extended poker.

Dad bounded from his chair, "Riley! You stop that, now!" Grabbing his outstretched arm, Dad dragged him to the door. "You'll have to get out of this house," he told the unresisting fellow.

After that, Fannie and I considered Riley a waking nightmare, whenever he went by our place. Evenings after dark were scariest of all. The clamor of his shouted songs and rattling cart carried far on the quiet night air before fading into eerie swamp echoes. Once, after being thoroughly frightened by Riley's noisy passing, Fannie and I lay trembling in our beds. After a bit, I began to drift toward sleep. "Mary, Mary, don't close your eyes," Fannie begged.

"Oh, I'm only resting my eyes," I said, trying to reassure my older sister. Good intentions were no match to my tired body, and before many minutes passed, I had left Fannie awake by herself.

Our dealings with Riley came to an end sometime after he threatened to kill Mom and brother Alvin. News of that and his otherwise strange behavior reached the ears of the Currituck County sheriff, who took Riley away to an insane asylum-a mental health facility today.

By the time I was twelve, a number of unhappy changes were taking place in our home. One, however, had what I considered its bright aspects. Mom and Dad were no longer church members, and starting seventh grade, Mom allowed me to wear non-Amish clothes. The new pink skirt and cardigan sweater made me feel smart and grownup. Gazing at the reflection in our bedroom mirror, I liked the face staring back: full lips, pensive blue-gray eyes set in an olive-skinned face, and dark braids neatly wrapped about the head. A rush of joy, mingled with some unnamed emotion welled up inside. Maybe, boys at school would notice me, even one of the high school boys. The thought sent a delicious shiver down my back.

That year, as well as the year before in sixth grade, there were times I rather enjoyed school. Sometimes girlfriends would come along home after classes. We'd sit around the kitchen table, sipping milk and eating thick slabs of Mom's home-baked bread, spread with apple butter or blackberry jam. Likely, Mom overheard our giggles and schoolgirl chatter, or maybe there were other signs that disturbed her. Now and again, she would say, "Mary, you're *boova ferookt*" (boy crazy). Whatever the reasons, Mom took me out of school before my seventh grade was half finished. Taking me out of school may have restricted my everyday contact with boys, but Mom was unable to completely stifle my growing interest in those exciting creatures!

I quit school in 1940 when I was twelve and have always regretted that I was denied an education.

Although that ended my public school education, I later obtained a high school equivalency certificate by passing a G.E.D. exam. My college experience is limited to accounting, computer, and music courses taken over the years at our local Tidewater Community College.

Chapter 4
To Market, to Market

As I reflect on the varied influences that have molded me into the person I am today–next to my faith in Jesus Christ–I believe few things have played a greater role than plain, everyday hard work. Far back as I can remember, there were daily chores for which I was responsible. In fact, during childhood and adolescence, I felt part of being a good person depended on how well I did my work.

Certainly my most important responsibility, looking after little brother Atlee, became almost second nature. Being Mom's youngest, Atlee, nicknamed Bud, was close to her heart and often on her mind. Always busy at one or more of her constant tasks, Mom had little time to keep track of the baby. That was my job, and when Mom or an older sister asked, "Where's Bud? What's he doing?" I was expected to know the answers. Negligence brought a sharp reprimand, at best; a really serious infraction could mean time in the stair closet.

Bud was barely out of diapers, until I had the assignment, making sure his toilet duties were properly done. No inside bathroom meant several-times-a-day treks to the outhouse. Bud couldn't go by himself for a couple reasons. First he was unable to unbutton his homemade broadfall-style trousers and underwear–"B.B.D.'s" (B.V.D.'s), as we called them. When he had finished business, I needed to button him again. Besides, an outdoor privy was no place for a small child alone. Toddlers, and even older children, were known to have fallen through the toilet holes. The results, anything but funny, could range from dreadful trauma to death, if the unfortunate one was not quickly rescued.

Caring for Bud was just one of my chores. I took turns wiping dishes, when I was still too short to reach the dry sink. The handicap was easily remedied by having me stand on a stool. With that, I could dry dishes from the rinsing pan while an older sister washed.

Bud and I in 1936.

Dad had built the sink tall enough to be comfortable for Mom. The flat top and three-inch tall rim board, all around, were overlaid with sheet zinc. "Dry sink" was an apt name, for it had no water supply or drain. To do dishes, two large dishpans were set into the sink, and filled with hot water from the kitchen stove reservoir. Upon finishing, we dumped the dishwater into the swill barrel—our garbage disposal—where other inedible food refuse went. Every so often, Dad added bran middlings to the slop, and fed it to the hogs. We were into recycling decades before the term was even known!

I helped with house cleaning as I grew older. Mom, a stickler for cleanliness, insisted spring cleaning was not properly done, unless the wood-boarded walls and ceilings were scrubbed by hand. Soon as I was tall enough to reach overhead, I'd stand on a small table, while Mom handed up hot soapy rags. "You missed a place there in the corner," she might say, or as I plied the rinse rag, "There's a soap streak, just above your head."

Before automatic washers, doing laundry took more effort than one can imagine. Most Amish households today have ringer washers, powered with gasoline engines. We did not. We heated water outdoors in a black iron kettle, then soaked the heavily soiled clothes in hot water to loosen some of the grime, before hand scrubbing them on a corrugated washboard with homemade lye soap. Everything was wrung out by hand, rinsed in clean water, wrung out again, and finally hung out to dry. Doing laundry on a blustery winter day turned into a brutal exercise. Your hands, already red and tender from the water and soap, became exquisitely painful in the cold air, as you fumbled clothespins and wet laundry onto the clothesline.

Everyone contributes to keep a farm running efficiently: feeding chickens, milking cows, cooking, baking, and the other countless things Amish farm families do, without the aid of modern appliances. Sometimes, the work is best done by each person doing his or her assigned duties, without much interaction among family members. Other endeavors involve everyone to accomplish the task at hand. Weekly hog butchering was such an activity. It took all of us working together to complete the two-day job.

Mom and Dad began processing and selling pork products, several years after moving to Moyock. As effects of the Great Depression were being felt across the United States, the economic pinch also reached our community. A few Amish families, including my parents, dealt with the hard times by hauling their produce to Norfolk and selling it at the city's curbside market. Venturing into the world of commerce had not been Dad's intention when he left Ohio. The fertile North Carolina land and moderate climate promised a good living for the farm family who worked hard and managed well. As it turned out, hard work and sound management could not overcome the low prices paid for crop grains and live cattle during the 1930s. So other means had to be found to support a wife and seven growing children.

Raspberries were among my parents' early forays into direct marketing. While Dad looked after the cultivation of the plants and getting in hired pickers, he did not enjoy dealing with customers. As a result, Mom took on some of the sales' duties. She made periodic trips by train from Moyock, to sell the ripe fruit to Norfolk buyers. Unlike Dad, with his distaste for meeting the public, Mom thrived on this exposure to the outside world; her natural friendliness soon drew a body of loyal customers.

Though successful, the raspberry project had its drawbacks.

The fruit's brief season did not offer long-term income, and a good harvest also depended on adequate rainfall. If that came up short, so did the raspberry crop.

Slaughter hogs, on the other hand, could be raised year-round, with no worry over the weather. All we needed was a constant supply. Dad bought some from area farmers, but we also raised many ourselves. The growing pigs roamed free in a large lot, while the sows were confined to smaller pens. I enjoyed watching the newborn piglets nuzzling their mother, as she lay on her side, grunting contentedly. However, out on the lot, the hogs lived up to their image of all that is crude and slovenly-pushing and squealing, as they fought over corn and slop, and afterwards flopping down in the muckiest spot they could find.

In 1932, Mom, sister Malinda, and little Bud returned to Ohio for a visit with relatives. During their absence, Dad built our summer kitchen and a big combination slaughter shed and butcher shop. Ingenious at planning and making things, Dad equipped the building, so the work could be done as easily as possible. He constructed a metal scalding vat, with a firebox underneath in the open-sided slaughter shed. An overhead track ran into the thirty-by-thirty-foot butcher shop, which was enclosed with board siding. A large black iron kettle, also with a firebox, stood in the center of the concrete-floored room. Wooden work tables lined the east wall. Along the north wall, Dad built a twelve-by-twelve-foot insulated icebox with a massive lid that was raised and lowered by a rope and pulley device. A sausage grinder, lard rendering equipment, hand water pump, and bottle washer were other conveniences Dad had installed. The bottle washer, powered by a gasoline engine, was a valuable time saver, since we used pint and quart bottles for the cream and milk we sold from our ten-cow dairy herd.

Butchering day, Wednesday, began early. With a kerosene lantern for light, Dad went out first to light a fire under the scalding vat. As the water heated, he would check periodically to be sure it was hot enough before the hogs were killed and bled. The water needed to

My mother and her helper Mamie Felton on butchering day.

be just below boiling–hot enough so the hair could be scraped off, but not so hot as to cook the skin.

Dipping a several-hundred-pound hog into scalding water is not a task for weaklings. Dad, however, had made it fairly easy, with a crossed-rope sling, attached to an overhead block and tackle. With two persons, Dad or Mom and one of the hired men handling the guide ropes, the hog could be rocked and turned as necessary before being lifted out, ready for scraping the hide. The hide scraper, a half-moon shaped metal blade, set in a wooden handle, was usually wielded by Dad or the hired man. Unlike most slaughter animals, hogs are not skinned; therefore, the hair needed to be scraped from the hide. Cut off later, the skin was cooked, chopped, and used for souse and scrapple.

Once scraped, and the few remaining hairs singed off with a blowtorch, steel hooks were inserted into the front leg tendons. The porker was then pulled into a full hanging position, next to be pushed along the pulley track into the butcher shop. There, Mom waited to begin her work. By no means physically large, Mom was, nevertheless, strong-muscled and expert with a sharp butcher knife. Using quick, deft strokes, she slit the underbelly, taking care not to puncture the intestines. Within minutes, the internal organs were spilled out into galvanized washtubs; the stomach cavity washed out with fresh water; and the carcass cut in half, ready to be taken down and laid on the worktable.

Now, everyone not involved with other tasks, set to work with boning knives. While the less desirable parts could wait until next day for processing, the choice meat needed to be put into the icebox as quickly as possible. After the loin cuts, came the backbone, spare ribs, and slabs of fat for lard. The hams and shoulders were deboned for sausage meat.

Meanwhile, Mamie Felton, the hired lady, or one of us girls, prepared the chitterlings ("chitlin's"). The intestines were stretched, flushed with clean water, and scraped to remove what offal might remain, then put into saltwater to soak overnight. An old Southern phrase aptly described marketers of pork products: "They sell everything but the squeal." The John Troyer family was no exception to that. We wasted nothing.

On Thursday the leavings were made into scrapple, liver pudding, and souse. Dad would get a fire going early under the kettle in the butcher shop to cook the chopped up pigskin, feet, heads, and livers. That all needed to cook several hours. All the while, the sausage meat had to be seasoned, ground, and packed into thirty-pound metal cans and returned to the icebox. The chitterlings were removed from their overnight saltwater soaking and scraped, then cooked in a large double boiler on the kitchen stove.

Lest all this appears as so much drudgery, it was not. The work was actually a part of our recreation, and without it an important element would have been missing from our lives. There was often laughter and good-natured teasing during the day. Jokes were made by playing on words. For instance: in Pennsylvania German, *Sei shtill* is literally "Be still," a relatively mild command. However, *Sei shtill*, was, and still is, more often used in the context of "Shut up!" The person would retort, "*Sei hucka net uff shtiel, sie hucka uff die shwens und greisha.*"

The explanation goes like this: The plural of *pig* is also *Sei*. *Shtill* is changed to *shtiel*, the plural of chair (stool). *Sei shtiel* thus becomes "pig chairs," and translated the retort says, "Pigs sit not on chairs, they sit on their tails and squeal."

Deduct, defense, defeat, and *detail* lent themselves to another ditty. "De duck flew over de fence, de feet before de tail."

Our attempts at humor may seem trite and unsophisticated by today's standards; we, nevertheless, found them worth chuckling over, and that was all that mattered.

Once the meat in the big kettle was tender, the liver and meat scraps were ground and broth added. Some of this mixture would be sold as liver pudding, and the rest mixed with yellow cornmeal and cooked into scrapple. Souse was made from the broth, small bits of skin and meat, and seasoned with salt and pepper. Poured out into pans, the souse congealed into a semi-solid, clear loaf, dotted with pork morsels.

Lard rendering came last of all. After the scrapple was done and the big kettle carefully cleaned, the raw pork fat was dumped in and boiled. Mom had strict rules for the finished product. "Keep stirring, Mary. We don't want it to scorch," she would order. The fat cooked until much as possible had become clear liquid. It could not be left too long on the fire, lest it darken and lose some of its quality. Once removed from the heat, the mixture went into the lard press to remove the cracklings from the liquid. Drained into metal cans, the lard solidified, taking on its natural whiteness. Snow white lard was one of Mom's specialties for her Norfolk market clientele.

Market day began early Friday morning. Well before daylight, Tom Sullivan, or sometimes Levi Slabaugh, would arrive with his car, towing a trailer. The boxes from the icebox were loaded aboard, and Mom, often with one of my older sisters, would set out for the twenty-odd mile trip to the city. In the early years, Mom had an outdoor stand along Brewer Street. The only protection against inclement weather was a canvas canopy, and a kerosene heater to warm oneself during winter's cold. Later, Mom moved into the Norfolk City Market building. This large, high-ceilinged structure was a major improvement over Brewer Street's curbside; nevertheless, it could not begin to compare or compete with the clean and well-lighted post–World War II supermarkets. That, and stricter rules by the health department, brought about Norfolk City Market's demise in the mid-1950s. It also ended an era that saw many changes taking place in the John Troyer family.

CHAPTER 5
The Rising Tide

MOST OF us know, things are seldom what they appear at first glance. Standing at an ocean beach, the unfamiliar observer could well conclude, that all the waves' energy is shoreward. The greatest apparent danger would lie in being knocked down and tossed high and dry on the sand. However, that is not the reality. Wading into the surf, the careless bather risks his life with an invisible force: undertow. While the surface wave is incoming, the water underneath is rushing seaward. Depending on tide and wind conditions, a powerful undertow can drag the strongest swimmer to his death.

Spiritual and emotional undertow describes, I believe, what happened to the John Troyer family. Beneath the surface appearance of a happy, God-fearing home, powerful forces were dragging us into deep water. My older siblings may have known earlier, but I was ten or eleven, before I realized something might be seriously wrong. Until then, I basked in the protective comfort of home and parents.

Certainly, childhood was not perfect. Some of the discipline meted out by our parents was abusive by today's standards. At the time, though, I accepted it as part of growing up. There was the rare sentence to the stair closet from Mom, but except for one occasion, I do not remember her as cruel or unjust. This particular incident sprang from my desire to be on good terms with everyone. I had sided with a family member over something, then took the opposing view with the other sibling. Mom's open-handed smack stung my cheek, but her words, "Mary, you two-faced thing," left a wound far more painful than the physical hurt.

Dad took a less active role in my discipline. Infrequently, I caught the end of the switch for a table infraction. More often, he scolded us after Fannie and I had gone to our room for the night. *Mayd, sind shtill!* ("Girls, be still!").

There may have been cracks in the foundation earlier, but my wall of serenity began crumbling one Saturday evening after

Mom returned from the market in Norfolk. Brisk sales for the two days had brought her one hundred dollars profit–a significant sum in those Depression years. Waving the bills in her clenched fists, Mom all but danced with excitement. "Look here, all this money I made at the market!" she exclaimed.

Dad reached for the money, "Here, Mom. Give it to me," he ordered.

Mom drew back, half giggling and shaking her head. "Huh uh, it's mine. I worked hard for this."

Dad threw his arm around her neck and pulled her to him, and began what I thought was a playful tussle. It all ended quickly, with Dad holding the money, as Mom backed away, laughing. They had done that before in front of us children, so it didn't seem terribly unusual at the time. I realized later, though, the emotion and intensity in that struggle amounted to more than simple fun.

Long afterward, I also understood why we were so unprepared for events that followed that encounter. Mom and Dad never shouted or argued in our presence. Along with that, whenever the two disagreed in our presence, she would respond with laughter. We children, as a result, saw what must have been serious differences between them as little more than Mom having fun with Dad.

I also know now, there were other danger signals we did not see at the time. For a few years, already, Mom had been making statements implying she did not consider Dad the ideal husband. She grew increasingly impatient over his lack of interest in the farm work. Sometime after 1936, he began work on developing a small, compact grain combine. Renting shop space in Moyock village from Mister Basnight, Dad and brother Alvin spent countless hours there, putting together a machine that he was certain would one day make our family wealthy. He promised, "When I get my invention done and patented, we'll have it good. I'll get electric in here, and you won't have to work at the market anymore."

Mom was sure he was wasting time, that might have been far better used, tending crops and helping with the barn chores.

Tiresome as those complaints became, they were far less distressing than her comments about her and Dad's marital relations. Though I understood little of what she was talking about, I cringed inwardly whenever she got on the subject. Somehow, it didn't seem decent that our mother was talking so explicitly to her daughters about their Dad.

Unfortunately, outside factors were also having their ill effect on our home. At a time when we needed the fellowship and active support an active church can give a family in crisis, the Moyock Amish colony was in the last stages of coming apart. From its beginning in 1918, the church had struggled with ongoing problems; by the mid-1930s, full decline had set in. Several families moved to the Kempsville and Deep Creek, Virginia, communities, while others went to Delaware and Ohio. No one came to take their places. When regular monthly services were no longer held at Moyock, Mister Cooper and other neighbors were hired occasionally to take some of the young people and men to services at the Deep Creek Amish Church. The forty-miles-plus round trip was too much for horse and buggy in a single day. As a result, months sometimes went by that Mom and we younger children spent Sundays at home.

The church breakup resulted from several reasons. Except for a year or two, Moyock always lacked a resident minister-a prime necessity for a thriving Amish community. During much of its existence, the congregation depended on the bishop, Dan Stutzman, from Deep Creek, or one of the Kempsville ministers to come monthly to preach and maintain discipline. Resulting disagreements over Amish rules added to some of the problems.

Toward the end, surrogate ownership of pickup trucks became an especially contentious issue. It worked this way: an Amish farmer would buy a truck for a neighbor or acquaintance, who could not afford to own a vehicle. Outwardly, both parties gained advantages, the Amishman bypassed the church *Ordnung* (rules) by not having the truck in his personal possession, yet the vehicle was more readily accessible than one owned by the hauler.

The driver also gained status among friends and family with his newly acquired pickup. The practice caused much controversy but went on for several years, both at Moyock and Kempsville. While not condoned, it did not bring immediate loss of church membership, as would the purchase of an automobile.

By 1937, Dad had grown increasingly concerned about this matter. Choosing not to take a roundabout way to car ownership, he bought his first Chevrolet that year, and began to drive. While I do not remember the exact time and details, buying the car was the main reason Mom and Dad were soon afterward excommunicated from the Old Order Amish.

Long before that occurred, tensions had existed between Mom and the church. Far back as her youth in Montana and Wisconsin, she could not have endeared herself to the guardians of Amish discipline. Though the small western communities may not have enforced the rules as strictly as the Amish did in Holmes County, Ohio, even out west, Dena Miller must have crowded the fences. Her dark blue wedding dress proved that. The perky little shoulder puffs and extra tucks and pleats on the cape, would raise eyebrows and bring a reprimand in some Amish circles yet today.

There must have been other incidents at Moyock, that brought disaffection between Mom and the church, but one in particular left a lasting wound. My older sisters were told by a couple of girlfriends, their father had sexually abused them. Malinda and Lizzie quickly relayed the story to our mother. Appalled, Mom tried to deal with the situation by taking it before the church. The fact that Dena Troyer, of all persons, was bringing the accusation was further complicated by the lack of resident ministers and bishop- which may not have made a difference in the end.

In the ensuing turmoil, the girls middle-aged father vehemently denied the evil deeds, thereby intimidating his daughters into silence. Mom, already marked as a less-than-faithful member, came away as a troublemaker and liar in the view of others in the congregation.

Although various factors contributed to our parents'

worsening marriage problems, I believe none played a greater role than Mom's years of market attendance in Norfolk. There she became acquainted with a world far different from the plain, separate religious life she had previously known. For the first time ever, others noticed and praised her special talents and abilities. "Oh, Mrs. Troyer, your home-baked bread is wonderful. Your pork sausage is the best we've ever eaten. Your cream is so rich, my husband won't let me buy it anywhere else."

And the compliments did not end there. Mom was lauded for the boundless energy and fast pace she maintained throughout a workday. She loved the recognition, and sometimes the men's flattery was positively exciting. "You're a fine lookin' woman, Mrs. Troyer. Mighty fine."

"Forty years old, and seven children? Really? Dena, you don't look a day over twenty-five." A few of the newfound friends skipped the "Mrs. Troyer," for more intimate terms. It was heady stuff.

Mom had come from a culture where personal compliments were rare. Praise for one's accomplishments was seen as the seed for pride-a cardinal sin. Work needed to be done "as unto the Lord, and not unto men." As for beauty, the inner loveliness that brings praise to the Creator, is far more desirable than outward, physical charms that draw attention to the created. But by then, Mom had scant interest in spiritual matters. Middle-age was no longer approaching, it had arrived. If she was ever to find the brand of happiness her worldly friends enjoyed, she must grab it now. How different the future might have been had Mom allowed God's will to control her life!

A year or two after Dad bought his car, Mom bought one also, a Ford coupe. The car gave her a dual advantage–independence from riding with someone else to Norfolk on market days, as well as the freedom to go where and when she pleased. That quickly added to the tensions between our parents. "Where are you going?" Dad would ask, evenings when she had dressed to go away.

"I'm going to visit . . . ," she'd say, naming one of her new friends.

"Mom, I don't like it. Just stay home with me and the

children," he'd beg. "It's not right for you to go out alone at night."

"Well, I'm going, Ruth is expecting me, and I'll be back before too late," she would defiantly insist.

More than half a century has passed since, but sister Fannie still recalls the hurt in Dad's face, as Mom closed the kitchen door behind her, and moments later the Ford rumbled to life.

Bud and I next to mom's Ford coupe, circa 1940.

Before our parents lost their church membership, rumors circulated that Mom had been unfaithful to Dad. At this late date, I have no reason to believe the stories were anything more than idle speculation, resulting from Mom's easy banter with "English" men. Flirting never was, and still is not, acceptable behavior for an Amish woman.

Coming at a critical time, the excommunication seemed to accelerate forces already in motion. Over the years, Mom sometimes stayed overnight Friday's at a downtown Norfolk hotel to avoid the late evening trip home and return to the city early the following morning. Then, we saw it simply as a convenience for our busy, hardworking mother. However, eventually, we would discover there was much more than that–so much, in fact, that our family would be changed forever.

With its Hampton Roads harbor considered one of the world's finest, Norfolk has been an important seaport since early colonial days. At the onset of World War II, the area boomed; but even before, the threat of the coming conflict drew job seekers from distant places. Many came to work at area shipyards, others as military personnel on station, and later on their way to land and sea battles in Europe or the South Pacific.

Among the throngs came a handsome thirty-year-old long-distance truck driver, Vernon Beard, from Fayetteville, North Carolina. He may have stopped by Mom's market stand as a customer;

or possibly, they were introduced by a mutual acquaintance. I never learned the details, but to my dismay, *divorce*–a frightening new word–began cropping up in Mom's conversations. Citing advice from one of her friends, she would say "Joan says I shouldn't put up with a man like him. She keeps telling me I need to get a divorce. Maybe, I will. It's just no use going on this way. All his talk about big money from his invention doesn't amount to anything."

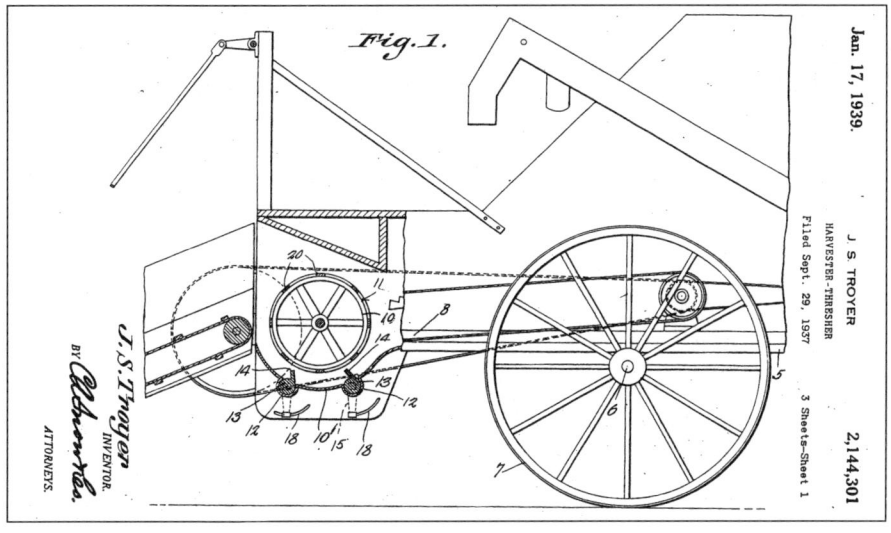

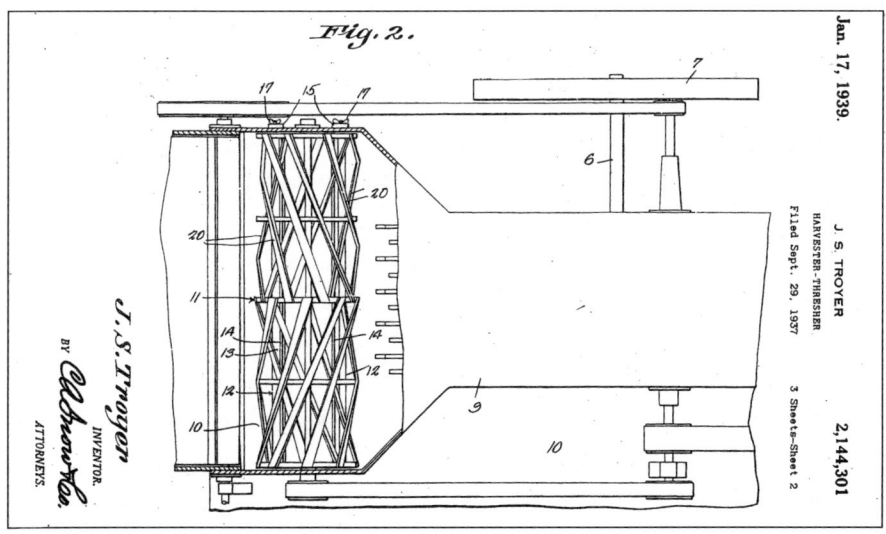

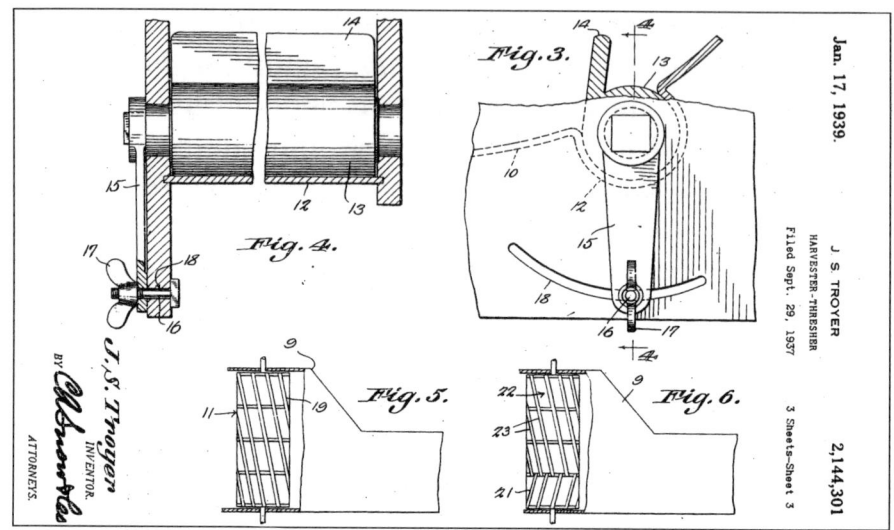

Dad had proven in early 1939, his work at the shop in Moyock had not been wasted effort. That year, January 17, he obtained a patent for his new threshing cylinder for grain combines. He sold the rights to the patent to the Massey-Harris farm equipment company. Dad would receive a royalty on each machine the factory produced.

"We'll have it made now," he loved to say, excitement rising in his voice. "Just wait 'til the checks start rolling in. After we get electric here on the place, I'll buy you a wash machine and a Frigidaire."

Somehow, the promise of future wealth could not bridge the rift in our family. Mom continued her talk of divorce. Dad must have known she was being unfaithful, and had no intention of quitting the affair. He left in 1940 and moved to a farm at Hickory, Virginia, ten miles away. Mom paid him two thousand dollars for his share of the farm at Moyock. The separation left me with a terrible emptiness inside. So much I had cherished, now swept away. Dad still came regularly to take Bud and me to Mount Pleasant Mennonite Church, where he and we had begun to attend. But I was so sad, our family was no longer together as before.

If the rumors were unkind before our parents' marriage breakup, they became even more meanspirited after Dad left.

People repeated gossip about "that Dena Troyer," in our very presence. Occasionally, I wanted to run screaming, "Stop! Stop! That's not true! I know it's not true! Why are you saying those awful things about my mother?" Of course, I never confronted anyone.

The stories fed the vicious cycle: the more people talked, the less Mom cared. She cut and permed her hair-a far step beyond local Mennonites' tolerance at the time. To further prove her growing sophistication, she began smoking cigarettes and using swearwords in conversation. While some earthy terms had been part of our Pennsylvania German, I never grew used to the coarse, vulgar English words coming from my mother's lips. In one final gesture of contempt for all she was leaving behind, Mom burned her Amish wedding dress.

My parents' divorce became final in 1941, the year I turned thirteen. Sister Edna married Francis Miller that year. The newlyweds moved in with Dad at Hickory. That left Fannie, Bud, Mom, and me on the farm. With the help of Mamie Felton's son Bruce, besides another black man and several women, Mom continued to butcher hogs and attend market.

About that time, I was becoming aware of the other man in Mom's life. Tall, blonde, and muscular, he cut a handsome figure. His blue eyes and dashing style may have captivated my mother, but I took an instant disliking to Vernon Beard. In my adolescent opinion, he was the reason Dad no longer lived in our home.

Vernon began coming to our place soon after the divorce. I was always uncomfortable in his

My mother and I in 1942.

presence, and could hardly wait until he would leave again. With all that was taking place, my childhood security had shattered irreparably. Sometimes I wondered if I would ever be happy again. Next to Vernon being at our place, I dreaded when Mom would drag

Bud and me along to her friends' parties. Everyone was always noisy, with a lot of coarse talk going on. The beach parties at Ocean View on Chesapeake Bay were emotional torment for me, and one incident bordered on cruelty.

Because we almost never went to the ocean or bay beaches as small children, the huge expanse of water was less than reassuring. There were seldom large waves, but simply wading to my waist became an adventure in itself. This particular time, I was in barely two feet of water, when Vernon began saying he would teach me to swim. "Come on, I'll show you how. It's easy," he coaxed.

"No," I shook my head and turned away. Learning to swim didn't excite me, and I especially did not want Vernon to be my teacher.

Suddenly, he grabbed me from behind. "Close your mouth and don't breathe," he ordered. Failing in my fright to heed the warning, the next instant I was swallowing saltwater. Though I fought desperately to get away, my puny strength was no match for his. He held me underwater until I was certain of drowning. When he finally released me, I came up nearly hysterical, sputtering, gasping, and crying all at once. Unfortunately, the ordeal didn't end there; the humiliation became worse when everyone laughed, including Mom. She said, "Oh, Mary, don't be a baby. Vernon was only playing. He wouldn't hurt you."

Regardless what Vernon intended, the incident left a deep impression. I believe it may be one reason the beach has never held much attraction for me since. While some persons can leave pressing duties for an outing at the shore, I find baking cinnamon rolls in the security of my kitchen far more appealing.

Chapter 6
Tears by Turns

THE SMALL black print screamed its silent message, where the yellow page lay open on the kitchen table. Mom sat slumped over, body shaking, and head buried in her arms. The heartbreak in her agonized sobs was like nothing I had ever heard before from my mother. True, recently, she had seldom laughed and sung the way I remembered from early childhood. Sister Fannie and I, however, could never have imagined the utter despair we were witnessing at the moment.

Maybe, this outburst of grief came from somewhere beyond this present tragedy. Was our Mom overwhelmed with sorrow for other more precious things lost or thrown away these past several years? I did not have the answer then, nor have I discovered it in the years since. While troubled by the depths of Mom's pain, Fannie and I found ourselves unable to sympathize, the way we might have under other circumstances. Later, Fannie would voice my own sentiment–harsh as the words now seem. "For so long, she made us cry. Now, it's her turn."

* * * *

Unless personally involved, one can not comprehend the distress felt by children who are caught in the midst of their parents' separation and divorce. When alienation and bitterness are driving your mom and dad in opposite directions, the anguish becomes all but unbearable.

In fact, from my experience, a close relative's death might have been less painful, than the trauma I experienced over the breakup of our home. When death takes a loved one, friends and the extended family surround us with their support and comfort. Difficult as the loss may be, if the loved one has lived for the Lord, we find solace in trusting the departed has gone to be with Jesus. Over time, raw emotions begin to heal, and one slowly returns to a semblance of normal life.

That did not happen for us. Like an open wound, reinjured

again and again, the hurt continued for years. Divorce was so rare among the Amish and Mennonites during the 1940s, that many treated it as the ultimate curse. While a few caring persons reached out to us children, most kept their distance, as though fearful of catching some dreadful disease.

Fortunately, sisters Edna and Fannie were there to help me get through the worst times. One particular occasion occurred shortly after Mom and Dad's divorce became final. I was struggling with that, Dad being gone, and other disruptions at home. Sister Malinda had married Roy Miller, and the couple had moved in with us at Moyock. Mom's boyfriend, Vernon Beard, came calling more often. Fourteen, at the time, I desperately wanted to leave, and didn't care whether I ever returned to this place, where life no longer made sense.

Sister Edna and husband, Francis Miller, were living with Dad at Hickory, across the Virginia line. Pregnant at the time, Edna asked Mom to let me come help her. While the request seemed reasonable enough to Mom, she didn't perceive at the time Edna and Francis' interest in me amounted to more than their need for a housemaid. As committed Christians, they had become increasingly concerned over my spiritual welfare and wanted me away from what they considered an undesirable environment at Moyock.

Since I was no longer in school, going to stay with Francis and Edna was easily accomplished. For several weeks I enjoyed the tranquility with just the four of us: Dad, Francis, Edna, and me. As I helped Edna with housekeeping and gardening, some of my emotional turmoil began to subside. I missed Fannie and Bud at times, though I saw them regularly at church.

All too soon, my growing calm was taken away. Mom concluded after a bit, that Francis and Edna were turning me against her. Knowing full well, gentle persuasion would not convince Francis, Edna, or me, that I should return to Moyock, Mom came up with another plan. Late one night, she arrived at Hickory with son-in-law, Roy. They apparently intended to get me out of my upstairs bedroom without anyone else being the wiser. Back then, country people rarely locked their doors at night, and Roy managed to slip into the house, while Mom remained in the car.

However, once inside, the plot went awry. Francis and Edna were awake and confronted the intruder. There was no violence, but the two men got into a serious discussion. as to why I should or should not go back to Moyock.

Stepping outside to continue the conversation, Francis called on his best evidence, that "Mary needs to stay here with us." In the warm summer darkness, Francis didn't notice the passenger in Roy's car with the window down. "I tell you what, that Vernon Beard is just no good. Back before Edna and I were married, she and Vernon were alone one night, comin' home from market. Don't you know, he tried to put his arm around her. Told her, 'I wish I was marryin' you, instead of your Mama.'"

Mom could not contain herself with that. Springing from the car, she pounced on the first thing handy-the dog's food dish. "I'll knock the stuffing out of you!" she screamed, and flung the pan in Francis' direction.

Edna and I would laugh over the incident in later years, but at that moment it was anything but funny. I cried, but in the end, we gathered my things and I went home with Mom and Roy.

Nothing had really changed there, and in no time I was back to the usual routine. After all, long as I could remember, every week followed the same pattern. Monday and Tuesday were for washing and ironing laundry, and anything else we could get done. Hog butchering came Wednesday and Thursday; Friday and Saturday were Norfolk market days. While Sunday gave us a brief reprieve, we always had farm chores: feeding animals and milking several cows.

During my early teens, Fannie and I seldom went along to market. Rather, we were left with housekeeping and end-of-the week cleaning responsibilities. On one of those days, an episode occurred that drew the bond between Fannie and me, even tighter. Though, thousands of miles have separated us at times, Fannie and I have maintained a special relationship from that day forward. She had been dusting in Mom's bedroom, while I was in another part of the house. Suddenly, my sister's loud cries set me running,

"Mary! Mary! Come here! Oooooh!'

Frightened by her evident pain, I rushed to find her leaning against the chest of drawers, and sobbing uncontrollably. "What, Fannie? What is it? What's wrong?"

Through a fresh burst of tears, she extended the paper in her hand. At first, I didn't understand what seemed to be an official document. Mom's name, Dena Troyer, was on it. Then, abruptly, comprehension dawned. "You mean . . .?" I choked, and burst into tears. Now, I knew the answer, full well. "This says Mom and Vernon are married! Oh, no!'"

Fannie and I clung to each other, as the full import sank in. Even though Mom and Dad were divorced, until now, my sister and I had nurtured the thought, weak though it was, that one day our parents would remarry, and we could be a family again. Finding the marriage certificate destroyed that hope. Together, we wept until there were no more tears–just, dry heaving sighs, that brought no release from our grief.

My mother in 1942.

We later concluded, Mom had intended that we find the certificate. Knowing the scene it would cause if she had told us personally, she chose to have us learn the hard truth by ourselves. Despite all the pain Mom's decisions caused, she was not heartless. There were times, in fact, I felt her concern for our emotional distress. Though she never consoled us with words, sometimes a glance or something in her presence told me she cared. Infrequently, she would present us with a frilly "English" skirt or blouse. We felt something of a guilty thrill wearing a garment that went beyond the Mennonite dress code of the day.

* * * *

World War II altered the lives of nearly all Americans, and we were no exception. The war may actually have been the main reason Mom married Vernon Beard. Sometime in 1942–43, he was drafted into the Army, and stationed stateside after boot camp. However, with the looming possibility of being sent overseas, he convinced Mom to marry him. In the event of Vernon being killed in the fighting, Mom, married, could receive an Army widow's benefits; otherwise, she would get nothing.

I knew few details at the time, and may have forgotten others, but I've learned since, Vernon was fearful of going into combat. He once told Mom in Fannie's presence, "I'd rather be a live coward than a dead hero."

As the massive buildup of men and arms for the invasion Europe grew apace, Vernon received his orders. Mom and Fannie took him to his station at Fort Belvoir, Virginia, in late 1942 or early 1943. Soon after, Mom began receiving letters from somewhere outside the United States. Though I can't be certain, I believe Vernon took part in the D-day landing at Normandy.

With Vernon gone, and nothing definite when he might return, Mom decided on a new course. She rented out our place at Moyock, and we moved over into Virginia, a few miles south of Great Bridge. The Heritage Farm had two large chicken houses, where we raised broilers. Raising broilers then, is what is called "labor intensive" today–we called it a lot of hard work. There was no automation, except a rubber hose to fill the waterers for several thousand squawking chickens. We poured buckets full of feed into narrow metal troughs, morning and evening.

For years, Mom's indulgence of Bud had been an irritation for us older children. Her leniency didn't change now, despite so much heavy work. Bud in his mid-teens, and though still in school, could very well have helped with the evening chores, but Mom never demanded much from him. He moped about as he pleased, with no direct responsibility to help around the farm. One serious habit of his, taking money from Mom's purse, would have had dire consequences for anyone else. However, Bud rarely drew so much as a reprimand for his infractions.

On one occasion, before we moved to Heritage Farm, Bud and I had gone along to market in Norfolk. While Mom was away from the register, I caught my brother swiping bills from the cash drawer. "Put that money back!" I ordered. "I'll tell Mom."

With a sly grin, he turned and ran, while I gave pursuit. We must have made quite a spectacle, I'm sure, chasing along Market Street, and me yelling, "Bud, you come back here! Right now!"

Heritage Farm's hardest job–cleaning out the chicken houses–came after the broilers were crated and hauled to the dressing plants. Fannie and I spent days shoveling out chicken litter. During warm weather, the clouds of dust turned to grimy smear against sweaty skin. Thirty minutes into the day's work, made last evening's shower seem a long time past.

* * * *

Despite my antipathy for Vernon, Mom did her best to help us connect with his family. She took Bud and me along to Fayetteville, North Carolina, to visit Vernon's mother and his brother, Sheldon. Mrs. Beard, a widow, was a sweet Southern lady. Soft-spoken and a Christian, she graciously hosted us in their home.

Sheldon and I were about the same age. Gentle-natured like his mother, Sheldon had none of his older brother's gruff personality, and spoke openly about his faith in Christ. Although, there was no romantic interest on my part, Sheldon and I became good friends during our visits there, and the time or two, he and his mother visited us. We met again, years later, when Sheldon introduced me to his family, a lovely wife and two children.

Having lost her once-happy disposition, Mom became ever more melancholy as time wore on. Nothing would amuse her. She never sang and seldom laughed. Sometimes, she'd stand, staring into space, far removed from her surroundings, away in some distant time and place. The one thing that lifted her spirits, mail from Vernon, came only on rare occasions. Months might go by with no word, then two or three letters would arrive on the same day.

One of the bright spots for us girls was Fannie's and my involvement with the young people's group at Mount Pleasant Mennonite Church. Back then, we depended on homemade entertainment. Watching a baseball game played by fellows from the community was a prime sports event for most of us–girls and ladies, especially. Television was not yet available, and even if it had been, Mennonite Church rules would not have permitted ownership–radios were barely tolerated in many congregations then. Fannie and I had gained some capability with accordion and guitar. While she and I played alone for our own enjoyment, eight or ten of us would often gather on evenings and Sunday afternoons, to sing and play at Emery Hochstetlers or another Mount Pleasant home.

Our music inspired Mom enough to spend fifty dollars–a princely sum at the time–for my seventeenth birthday. The gift was a guitarist's dream, a beautiful, blonde Gibson flattop. Strummed, the instrument gave forth full, rich sound, and I delighted with the feel of it in my hands. My favorite gospel and country tunes flowed so easily from the strings.

The pleasure with the new guitar turned out to be short-lived, however. One day about noon, scarcely two weeks after my birthday, someone knocked at our door. Mom opened to find a gentleman in military uniform standing there. Although, our first time for such a visitor, we knew immediately what his presence portended. After almost three and one-half years of war, a United States Army officer on your doorstep meant grim news. The man had not come to pay a friendly social call. He spoke, "Does Mrs. Dena Beard reside here?" Mom nodded, wordless.

"Are you Mrs. Beard?" the officer asked. Again, Mom nodded. "I'm sorry, ma'am, but I have a telegram here for you," he said, and held out an envelope.

Still mute, Mom took the letter and turned back to the kitchen. The color gone from her face, she sat down at the table and began tearing at the envelope. Mechanically, her fingers unfolded the single page. The terrible words were there, just as we knew they would be: "SECRETARY OF WAR DESIRES ME TO EXPRESS HIS DEEP REGRET THAT YOUR HUSBAND, VERNON BEARD, WAS KILLED 18 MARCH 1945, DURING COMBAT IN GERMANY. . . ." The message gave a few more details, and was signed by an adjutant general of Vernon's Army unit.

Mom sat trance-like for several moments, before giving in to her grief. At first, she wept silently into her hands, then put her head down on the table, as heavy sobs racked her body. Fannie and I wept with her. While we did not fully share her personal loss, it was painful, nevertheless, to witness our mother's extreme suffering. For one, whose efficiency, hard work, and strong will had always maintained control during a crisis, Mom was exposed and helpless in that moment, as I had never seen her before. By evening, her distress remained so great, Fannie had to help with her bath.

Days passed before Mom showed any signs of recovering from the news of Vernon's death. Since the body could not be shipped home until war's end, there was no funeral and none of the closure that usually goes with the passing of a loved one. Along with that, Mom had become an outcast from her Amish and Mennonite connections, and few persons came to offer the condolence and support, that are so much a part of the church community. Except for Fannie, Bud and me, Mom was mostly alone with her grief.

Gradually, time dulled the initial shock, and Mom began planning a future without Vernon in her life. "Girls," she said one day. "I've been thinking about it, and I know this broiler raising is just too hard work for us women alone. We'll quit here and move back to Moyock. With you and Bud helping, we can start over, butchering hogs and going to market again."

Much as she may have desired, Fannie and I weren't interested. It would put us miles farther from our social activities with the Mount Pleasant youth, and moving back to Chitlin' Switch was not appealing. Furthermore, Dad had recently made an attractive offer that we were inclined to accept. If Mom chose to go back to Moyock, she would do it without Fannie and me.

Chapter 7
Soul Guardians

THEY WERE there from my earliest childhood—persons who were concerned about my spiritual welfare. Like beacons in sometimes dark and stormy waters, their nurturing by gentle example and spoken reprimand pushed me onward toward Jesus, the true Light.

Grandma Malinda Miller impressed me, early on, with her devoted Christian life. Though, she and Grandpa Rudy moved away, before I started school, I have never forgotten her quiet unassuming presence and welcome smile when we visited. Later, I would learn about some of the hard things she had endured—eleven children dying in infancy; yet there was no hint of bitterness or self-pity. Instead, she took on the task of raising her brother Allen's daughters, Matilda and Lizzie, after their mother died. Even her last earthly years were full of sadness that her adult children were living outside God's will.

Despite little direct Bible teaching at home, our parents, nonetheless, instilled us with spiritual principles. No meal was eaten without the blessing asked and thanks returned afterwards. Like many Amish families, ours ended the workday with evening prayers. Those times were special to me. God seemed so near when we knelt for prayer.

Dad had an active interest in church life, and was especially concerned about the Moyock Amish congregation's dependence on visiting ministers for Sunday services. Believing our family and others in the community needed a more regular spiritual diet, Dad helped organize a Sunday school. While the group sometimes met at the old hotel on Puddin' Ridge Road, Dad apparently wanted a place closer home. Having rented farmland just down our road, he cleaned and painted an empty chicken house, and we with several more families began having Sunday school there.

The Sunday school's main purpose was that we learn to read

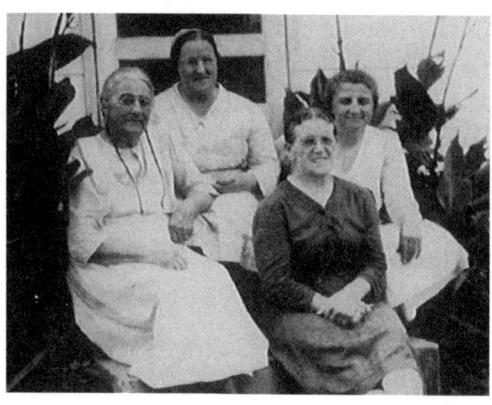

Left to right are James' grandmother Malinda Kemp, my Sunday school teacher Lydia Miller, Lydia's sister from Michigan, and my mother-in-law Naomi Bergey.

the Bible in high German. We children were first taught our *Ah Bay Tsays* (ABCs), then spell words and pronounce them from a German primer. Older youths and adults, taking turns, read from the Bible verse by verse. I do not believe teachers or students discussed what had been read. Interpretation of Scripture was considered a task only ordained ministers could do properly. Singing was always a part of Sunday school, and I learned the beloved children's song, "*Gott ist die Liebe*," there.

After most of the other Amish families had left the community, Sunday school was discontinued. Dad and my older sisters then attended Amish services at Deep Creek, Virginia. However, as I mentioned earlier, Mom, Bud, and I stayed home more often than not. About this same time, word of Mom and Dad's marital problems reached the ears of the ministers at Mount Pleasant Mennonite Church, at Fentress, Virginia. Clayton Bergey and Amos Wenger visited our home on several occasions. Although I have no memory of either of them speaking to me, other than possibly, "Hello," I knew their arrival was important for the way sisters, Edna and Lizzie, scurried to hide the battery-powered radio. Brother Bergey was a big man with a deep voice. Brother Wenger spoke in the direct, precise manner of an educated person.

Whether the two men came on their own initiative or by Dad's request doesn't matter. Their visits showed that someone cared about the unhappy events taking place in the John Troyer home.

Dad began taking Fannie, Bud, and me to Sunday services at Mount Pleasant, not long before he and Mom separated. He continued to provide our Sunday transportation after moving to Hickory, which obviously showed his concern for that aspect of our lives.

While my sense of security slipped away at home, I was, meanwhile, developing an attachment for the congregation at Mount Pleasant. At age thirteen or fourteen, I accepted Jesus as my Savior, and after a series of instructional classes was baptized, along with several more young people.

Over time, a number of persons would provide the spiritual nurture I wasn't receiving at home. Probably, more than anyone else, Lydia Miller led me to understand what being a Christian really meant. As young girls' Sunday school teacher, Lydia taught more than Bible stories. Having served in a missions program in Michigan, her home state, Lydia inspired us with a vision and call of service to others. Her beautifully hand-painted wall mottoes made Bible verses come alive, and her evident devotion to the Lord left an indelible impression on my young mind.

Almost from the beginning of my attendance at Mount Pleasant, Leona Miller and Dorothy Tennefoss became best friends of mine. Though sister Fannie and I were close, she was almost four years older, and I was too young then for her social group.

Because of my friendship with Dorothy, I spent many pleasant Sunday afternoons at the Tom and Mabel Tennefoss' home on Bedford Street. Occasionally, Dorothy's older sister Ruth bribed me into washing dishes for a penny. Yes, a penny. I know it seems incredible now, but that was 1941, a penny still had some worth, and furthermore, washing dishes went with mealtime as much as eating dessert.

Afterward, we rode bicycles, giggled, and talked about boys, and often joined several–Tommy Tennefoss Jr., Ivan Miller, Sammy Brunk, and the Hochstetler brothers, Milan and Carson, in a game of baseball. And it was baseball. Softball, back then, had no semblance to the popular game it has become today. Serious

My close friend Leona Miller and I.

ballplayers considered softball a game suitable only for girls and small children. Although, no religious training was involved, these sociable times, nevertheless, helped me establish ties to the Mount Pleasant congregation, that endure even today.

At the Francis B. Miller home, Leona's mother, Lena, served as gentle rebuker through most of my teen years. The admonitions were usually relayed by Leona, after Lena had heard about an escapade of mine. Lena didn't hesitate voicing her opinions, for she must have known her daughter would pass them along to me. She was definitely concerned about whom I might be dating. I believe she had decided by my late teens on a fellow from church, who would be a proper husband for me. However, to Lena's dismay, I made my own decision about boys I chose to date. Once, after learning I had dated a fellow from another state, Lena asked in exasperation, "Oh, what will Mary do next?"

While I sometimes may have been annoyed, I also knew Lena truly cared about me. Her comments, more than gossipy chatter, were meant for my spiritual betterment. One of her reprimands helped break my habit of using expletives–mild oaths, soft profanity, or whatever label one wishes to use.

Much as we disliked Mom's coarse language, Fannie and I had taken to using *gee, golly, gosh,* and *heck* in our everyday vocabulary. Without realizing, we had also fallen into a speech pattern others found offensive. One day, I let, "Darn it," slip out in Lena's hearing. Next time I saw Leona, she was ready with her mom's rebuke. "Mary, Mom says she wishes you wouldn't say *darn* and *gosh*. She says those words really mean 'damn' and 'God,' and that's taking God's name in vain. You know the Bible says we're not to do that."

Leona's words touched a tender spot, and their full impact was driven home a few days later while reading my Bible: "Out of the same mouth proceedeth blessing and cursing. My brethren, these things ought not to be." (James 3:10) King James Version.

Enlightened by this Scriptural verse and prompted by the Holy Spirit, I asked God's forgiveness and the strength to overcome. The struggle was difficult at first. Now and again, at an emotional moment, one of those old expressions popped out. However, I didn't give up. I believed God would help me, and He did. One day, months or maybe a year later, I suddenly became aware, those unnecessary words were no longer in my thoughts. I thanked God for the sweet victory. The experience taught me, we can sometimes refrain from a particular activity, because someone else disapproves, but only by God's grace and the power of the Holy Spirit is the urge taken from our minds.

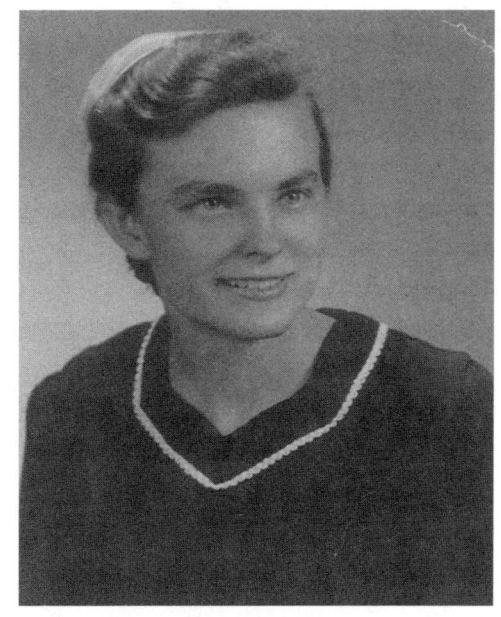

Leona Miller.

There were certainly other persons who influenced my spiritual development, but those mentioned here, along with sister Edna and her husband, Francis Miller, mentioned earlier all played important roles during a critical time of my life. Later, God would send a person into my life, who helped focus my eyes on Jesus Christ, as no other person had ever done before.

Chapter 8
Love's Promise

MOM BEGAN plans for returning to Moyock, soon after Vernon Beard's death. Fannie and I, however, decided we weren't interested in moving back to Chitlin' Switch. Our social life revolved around the Mount Pleasant community, and we didn't relish being several miles farther yet than the Heritage Farm. Besides, the place at Moyock had no electricity, and doing without it seemed an unnecessary inconvenience. Last, but not least, Dad had been encouraging us to come and keep house for him at Hickory. The most tempting part of his offer was the promise to buy each of us a new bedroom suite. As a result, by summer 1945, Fannie and I moved into Dad's ramshackle two-story house at Hickory, while Mom and Bud went back to Moyock, alone.

I can't describe all that I felt, moving in with Dad. Seeing one's father weekly at church is not enough to maintain a personal relationship, and over the past four years he had become less and less a central figure in my life. Now, in the mix of sadness for what we had lost, there was also a small, wavering hope, that our broken family might once again have a brighter future. For a number of years, Fannie and I rode a roller coaster of emotions—now up, then down—as Mom and Dad made overtures toward being reconciled. Eventually, though, all our best hopes would be in vain.

By now, Dad's invention was finally paying off. The Massey-Harris Company was sending a yearly royalty check of five to six thousand dollars. Though not a fabulous sum, it provided a good living in the years immediately after World War II. Dad bought a new Chevrolet car each model year with enough left over to engage in various enterprises that caught his fancy at the moment. To the outsider, John Troyer appeared to have reached his goals. The long years of striving had finally brought him a semblance of wealth.

Sister Fannie and I, however, were well aware even before we moved, our father had not found happiness and peace of mind with his apparent success. Instead, Dad was lonely and heartbroken, and felt castoff by most of his former acquaintances. An edge of bitterness crept into his tone, when he spoke about church matters. "The Amish put me out, and the Mennonites won't have me," he would say.

While Dad had continued to attend services at Deep Creek and Mount Pleasant Mennonite Churches for a number of years, the congregations would not accept him for membership because of his and Mom's divorce. He considered the policy unfair and reminded anyone who would listen, that Mom, not he, had filed for divorce. He cited, without success, the seventh chapters of Romans and First Corinthians as evidence that one should not be held responsible for an unbelieving spouse's behavior.

My sorrow for his pain became even more acute, as Dad increasingly turned to the bottle for comfort. Though he never drank openly in our presence, the evidence was there, nevertheless–the whiskey fumes and unsteadiness of foot–when I returned home late evenings after a date.

* * * *

Life in the United States a half century ago was far different from today. While a few self-service grocery stores existed, the huge supermarkets, shopping centers, and malls of the 1990s were things we could have scarcely dreamed. We had few of the devices that now take up our leisure time. Television had been invented, but few sets were available until the late 1940s; video games, stereos, and cassette players were still years in the future. Radio and movies existed, but Amish and conservative Mennonites saw them as worldly, unfit entertainment for faithful church members.

Despite the lacks and restrictions, we found ample opportunities for fun. As I described earlier, during childhood we played outdoors with cousins and neighbor children. By early teenage, though, I was looking forward to what many Amish and Mennonites of that era later remembered as the best part of growing up. That began at fifteen or sixteen, when one began participating in church youth group activities. It also meant you were old enough to start dating. Whether boy or girl, a first date marked an important milestone. It meant you were leaving childhood and stepping into the adult world. With that came a greater sense of ease among your peers. You now had a convincing reason to be a member of the group, other than just by virtue of being old enough.

Measured against today's countless things to do and places to go, my first date seems really insignificant; yet, it was typical of what a "date" meant then–Clarence B. escorted me home after a Sunday evening church service. I was sixteen and briefly staying with sister Edna and brother-in-law Francis who were living in the house along Maxwell Street where Melvin and Dorothy Wenger presently live.

Dates with different fellows came quite frequently after that. While I enjoyed the attention, I was not particularly attracted to any one fellow in the beginning. I do recall one date after turning seventeen. The boy, only fifteen, was painfully shy, and try as I might, attempts at drawing him into conversation were all but useless. I vowed afterward to stick with older fellows, and especially, someone who enjoyed conversation and laughter as I did.

At the time I joined the youth group, sister Fannie's popularity was already well established among a select circle of friends. Her position gave me easy access to this "in" bunch. The loose-knit clique of ten or twelve included a majority from Mount Pleasant and the Weaver brothers, Ernest and Herman, from the Kempsville (Beachy) Amish-Mennonite congregation. Also in the group was Bobby C. Of medium build and dark-haired, Bobby was a clean-cut young man, who didn't smoke or drink. What set him apart was that he came "from a non-Mennonite background." The term seems exclusive and insensitive by standards today; however, then, anyone who did not have Mennonite roots was tagged with the label. Despite his "outsider" status, Bobby C. readily gained acceptance in our circle with his fun-loving, friendly personality.

Fannie was at her best planning fun times. Sometimes on Sunday afternoons, we'd make homemade ice cream, mixing and cooking the custard, then hand-cranking a freezer until the frozen treat was done. On one such occasion, Homer Wenger cranked until he was certain no mere girl could budge the handle. He dared me to try. I grabbed the crank and turned, not once, but fifty more rounds to show Homer, and anyone else who may have doubted, some ladies do have arm strength!

Our common interest in country music–hillbilly, then-probably–more than any one thing held our group together. We had record collections of Roy Acuff, the Delmore Brothers, Grandpa Jones, and other Grand Ole Opry stars. Sunshine Sue was a favorite personality on Richmond's WRVA radio station. While listening to famous musicians was a favorite pastime, we enjoyed even more making our own music. True, some of the Mount Pleasant Church leaders were opposed to musical instruments, but that didn't stop us from playing at informal social gatherings.

I had learned to love the guitar as a ten-year-old, listening to my sisters sing and play with a few of the Moyock Amish young people. Over the years, I had taught myself a few simple chords, but had not become an accomplished guitarist until I met Bobby C. Two years older than I, he thrilled me from the beginning with his mastery of the instrument. Could I ever learn to do those bass runs, coming so effortlessly from the strings? Maybe, he would teach me. I hoped so.

I didn't have long to wait before Bobby was teaching me guitar. He apparently enjoyed sharing his musical knowledge with me. "Here, Mary, it goes like this," he'd say, breaking into an easy grin, and brown eyes twinkling. Nimble fingers danced across the frets, as the guitar thumped a rhythm to match my own pounding heart. Watching and listening as best I could, I tried to follow on my own Gibson flat top. There were times, however, I found myself distracted when I caught a glint of something special in Bobby's eyes.

He and I began dating occasionally, while Fannie and I were still living with Mom and Bud on the Heritage Farm, but I continued to date other fellows, until late summer 1945. By then, Bobby and I were serious enough to agree to go steady. Meanwhile, we continued participating in some Mount Pleasant Church activities. I went to Sunday morning church services, and he sometimes joined me for the evening meeting.

Bobby came from a Pentecostal background, but to my knowledge, never showed much interest in his family's church life. In fact, all during our courtship, I never met his parents or visited in their home. I did meet his older sister once or twice and learned rather quickly, she did not favor having a plain Mennonite girl as a sister-in-law.

If music was the bond that held our group of friends, then much more, playing our guitars and singing strengthened the love between Bobby and me. He sang lead and I sang alto. We developed quite a repertoire. Fannie and I, earlier, had sung mostly gospel songs, "Heaven," and "Jesus, Hold My Hand," were particular favorites. While Bobby and I included those in our duet, we also enjoyed doing "Daddy's Whiskers," "Wildwood Flower," "Turkey in the Straw," and "Guitar Boogie." Now and again, Bobby would laughingly say, "Mary, if we get married and have children, they'll have to love guitar music; else, we'll give 'em away."

As our music improved, the compliments from our friends became more profuse. "You guys are good!" "I could listen all day and night." "You should be on the radio."

Bobby and I talked about future possibilities, performing at special events: private parties, festivals, and country fairs, and maybe, even our own radio show. It was exciting to dream! Of course, we would stay away from nightclubs and other disreputable places. Years afterward I would learn how idealistic and naive I had been as a seventeen-year-old.

Fannie's and my one brief venture into the local nightlife is humorous in retrospect. We had gone with our fellows to a country barn dance. Who should be there but Harold Clendenning! Harold, though not a Mennonite, knew the rules full well. He came on like a beagle after timid bunnies. "What're you two doin' here?" he demanded. "You look like fish outta water. This is absolutely no place for a couple of Mennonite girls."

Needless to say, the good time we had anticipated turned into a guilty embarrassment.

The months passed and as my interest in Bobby grew, I became less involved with the church at Mount Pleasant. Sometimes on Sunday evenings, we would drive to the Kempsville community, after the Amish–Mennonite young people's singing had ended around 9:00 p.m. Even though, the ministers there had a much dimmer view of musical instruments yet, than Mount Pleasant leaders, the Weavers–Ernest and Herman–and often several more would get together for our music.

On other occasions, Bobby and I double-dated, sometimes with Fannie and her fellow, Tommy, or another couple of friends. We would head to the amusement park at Ocean View or off to a movie in Norfolk. At the time, there were no theaters closer, and one needed to drive to the city to see a movie. In early childhood, we were taught "picture shows" are sinful, and Dad would never have permitted us to attend. However, after he and Mom separated, she sometimes allowed Bud and me to see an afternoon show on a rare Saturday, when we had gone along to market. As a result, I now had little conviction against going with Bobby, though movies were still off-limits for Mount Pleasant Church members.

I have long since forgotten the scenes from those old movies, but one unhappy memory stands out sharply. That was the night my lovely, and almost new, Gibson guitar was stolen. Car trunks of that time had to be key locked after closing. Unfortunately, Bobby failed to do that before we entered the theater. I was positively devastated when we returned to find my cherished birthday gift gone forever.

* * * *

Sometime around New Year 1946, Bobby and I became engaged. We did not set a date, but talked about our wedding, "maybe, in the fall." Because church rules at Mount Pleasant did not permit any personal jewelry, instead of the usual diamond, Bobby gave me a fine wristwatch to mark our engagement.

Thrilled as I was to wear this token of our love, I discovered soon enough not everyone was happy with my decision. A best friend, Leona Miller, told me her mother, Lena, was disappointed in the direction I was taking. An all but public reprimand came from brother-in-law Francis Miller. The Mennonite Central Committee's meat canner was in the area at the time, and the Mount Pleasant Church group had gathered for the annual meat-for-relief canning project. There, someone remarked about my new watch, and Francis, never one to mince words, spoke up, "Yeah, I think Mary's makin' an unwise decision, marryin' this non-Christian fellow."

Francis' blunt comment left me wondering, why were persons whom I respected so negative about our engagement? Didn't they want me to be happy? Obviously, they didn't know what a fine young man Bobby really was.

Allow me to be forthright here about something I consider very important. Although, Bobby had a less than active interest in church life, and I was spiritually adrift, we did not become sexually intimate during our courtship. He was a decent, moral fellow, and I, while only seventeen, had high ideals about keeping my virginity for marriage. In light of all that had occurred in the John Troyer family, some readers may find that statement difficult to believe; particularly, those who have grown up midst the rampant promiscuity that marks our culture in recent decades. I can hear the skeptical comment, "But look at what your mother did. How could you avoid anything less?"

Here is sister Fannie's answer when asked that question in recent years. "At the time, a lot of people considered us wild and loose. But, regardless what others thought, Mary and I were determined not to allow boys to do anything that we might be sorry for later."

Several reasons bolstered that resolve. First, as mentioned earlier, times were different then, and a girl's good reputation was something to be protected. There was the social stigma–near disgrace–with an out-of-wedlock pregnancy. Modern contraceptives were not available, and even had they been, few physicians would have prescribed them for a young single woman.

More importantly, as Mennonite young people, we were regularly admonished about Biblical courtship standards. At spring and fall revivals, the visiting evangelist nearly always set aside one evening to speak specifically to the young people.

Back of all those factors was also the clear awareness that in spite of Mom's own sad example, she and Dad wanted Fannie and me to be "good girls." While I could not have consciously identified everything affecting my life then, I thank God today for sending those restraints that helped me make good moral choices as a teenager.

CHAPTER 9
The Commitment

As the weeks passed, there came a gnawing uneasiness over my engagement to Bobby C. It was something I couldn't quite name. Yet, looking forward to our wedding and future married life, somehow, I didn't have the fluttery excitement brides-to-be are supposed to experience. Some of my trepidation came, no doubt, from the grim reality of Mom and Dad's failed marriage. Much as I could, I pushed those unhappy memories out of my mind. Our marriage had to succeed! I wanted that with all my heart and would do everything in my power to make it happen. Besides, Bobby was a considerate man, and together, we would share the task of making a happy marriage.

Despite my effort to keep the doubts at bay, too often, a sneaky "what if" would creep in, and my heart would flutter momentarily. Why was I having such dumb thoughts, I wondered? The struggle lasted through late winter and early spring 1946.

That year, Deep Creek Mennonite held its annual two-weeks revival in April. Deep Creek and Mount Pleasant were, and still are, part of the Virginia Mennonite Conference. A dozen miles separate the congregations, and with southeast Virginia's relatively small Mennonite numbers, the two have long shared church activities. The revival, in fact, was typical of the ties that existed at the time. Mount Pleasant held its meetings in the fall and Deep Creek planned theirs for spring. As a result, the hosting congregation could expect strong support from the other group.

Turnout that year went far beyond the usual. Described later as "the greatest revival ever at Deep Creek and beyond," people crowded into the small sanctuary, jamming pews, filling the aisles with folding chairs, and finally, standing along the walls.

Andrew Jantzi, a young evangelist, from upstate New York, conducted the evening services. Preaching in the blunt, straightforward manner of old-time revivalists, Brother Jantzi captivated the audience with true-life stories—sometimes humorous, sometimes sad—to teach Bible principles. If the stories failed to hold one's attention, his resounding hand slaps and thumping foot stomps kept even the most careless from nodding off. That his style brought results was proven by the number of persons responding to the invitation at the end of each service.

Sister Fannie and I attended the meetings together, as we were living at Hickory then, and it took only a night or two for Brother Jantzi's words to stir my emotions.

"My dear friends, I maintain if anyone has the right to be happy, it's the child of God. Outside of Jesus Christ, you'll never find real happiness. Listen, young folks, you may think running with the old crowd will make you happy. Or maybe, this very evening, you're looking forward to marriage with that special young man or woman, believing you'll find happiness there. I'm here to tell you unless Jesus Christ has control, you'll be miserable the rest of your life.

"Listen to me," he commanded, index finger stabbing at the audience. "It's an awful thing to die without Christ, and be cast into eternal hell. The Gospel of Mark, chapter nine, verse forty-four, tells us plainly, 'Where their worm dieth not and the fire is not quenched.' It's terrible to think, at the end of the road all you have left is eternal hell to look forward to."

I could feel my heart pounding. Talk of hell always frightened me, and Jantzi's vivid portrayal left me trembling. While I desired happiness here on earth, I wanted heaven even more when my life ended.

With his sermon over, the evangelist announced, "I'm going to ask our chorister now to lead us in the invitation hymn, and while the congregation sings, we invite you, sinner, backslider, young or old to come forward. There are personal workers waiting to pray with you."

"That's right, that's right, brother. Just step right out," Jantzi coaxed. "God loves you. The Holy Spirit is saying, 'Come, come on.' God bless you, young ladies. Yes, yes, come forward."

Fannie and I were caught up in the intensity of the moment. She stirred beside me and whispered, "I'm going."

Our growing closeness the past several years usually found her leading and me following. It was no different now. The moment she got up from the pew, I was a step behind her. Tears stung my eyes, as a strength greater than my own drove me down the aisle, while the congregation sang, "Just as I am, Thou wilt receive, wilt welcome, pardon, cleanse, relieve. . . ." Yes, the words expressed my longing exactly: to be received by the Lord and relieved of the uncertainty I had struggled with in recent months.

An older lady knelt with me as I cried and prayed, "Oh, God, I want you to be first in my life. Take away whatever would keep that from happening." After the prayer, the lady murmured brief encouragement–words I have long forgotten. However, the freedom and lightness, as though my feet were barely touching the floor, are so deeply etched in my memory, that I will remember so long as I keep my rational mind. There was also the assurance that if I were to die that night, I would go to heaven. Being a new person in Christ had become a reality for me.

The public commitment marked an important milestone in my life, but it was only the first of several important decisions I would make over the next few years. Difficult as those choices often were, time has confirmed that God was leading my every step.

One day shortly after the revival, I read a gospel tract during my personal devotions. The tract had been given to me by Lydia Miller. As I thought about its message on the Christian home, I was suddenly overwhelmed with the sense of God's presence there in the room. What I did next was new for me. I stood and talked with God. I had prayed since childhood: at home in the evenings when Dad read from the German prayer book, at church while the congregation knelt, and privately when facing a troublesome circumstance, this was different.

While those experiences sometimes moved and inspired me, this conversation with God reached deep into my soul, as I told Him, "God, You know how much I hate divorce, how much pain it has caused our family. More than anything else, I want a Christian husband and family, a home where our children will love and serve You."

It wasn't eloquent or lofty, but I meant the request with every fiber of my being. Though God did not reply in an audible voice, I was confident He had heard. Exactly how and when it would all come about did not concern me so much as my desire to reach the goal. The most important thing for now was learning to know His will and being obedient to it. I knew God would not fail me.

Fannie was going steady with Tommy at the time of the Deep Creek revival. Earlier, he had begged her to marry him. Though fond of Tommy, Fannie had refused his proposals, but had not broken off the relationship. Following her public commitment, however, she quickly made up her mind. "Mary, I'm going to quit Tommy. We've had some good times, but he smokes and likes a beer, now and then. He's not saved, and I can't keep on with him any longer. When it comes to marriage, I want a man I know is a Christian."

It was characteristic of my sister to promptly reach a decision and act on her convictions. It wasn't nearly so easy for me, especially, when another's feelings were involved. Growing in my Christian life, I had begun to understand the anxiety over my engagement to Bobby was more than just a bad memory, left over from the breakup of Mom and Dad's marriage. While I had lacked spiritual insight, I well knew, Bobby had never shown much interest in living an active Christian life. Decent and moral though he was, we never prayed or read the Bible alone together.

In fact, it would have stretched the imagination to picture us kneeling for prayer, the way our family did when I was a child at home.

As the weeks went by, I began to feel tugged, first one way and then another. Bobby loved me and I was sure I loved him. Otherwise, I would not have become engaged in the first place. Surely, we had enough in common to be a compatible couple. Our music alone would hold the bond between us. After all, playing our guitars and singing had brought us together in the first place, and certainly that would help keep us together in the future. Bobby had a good sense of humor and loved to laugh and joke. which I also enjoyed. Somehow, the logic couldn't quiet an inner voice that grew ever more insistent: "Remember, Mary, you asked for a Christian home and family. Will Bobby be a Christian husband?"

Much as I wished for a ready, solid "Yes!" I knew it wasn't there. Determined to do God's will, I was beginning to realize that a sincere follower of Jesus meets many obstacles along the way. Besides the voice from within, I was also getting Fannie's regular admonishments. "Mary, you know what you have to do. Don't keep putting it off. The longer you wait, the harder it will be. Bobby is not a Christian You know that, and you must break your engagement. You have to!"

Summoning the courage and following through became the most difficult thing I had ever done. Several months passed. By then, the matter involved more than Bobby's lack of Christian commitment. I had grown increasingly aware that I was not ready for marriage at eighteen. There were other things to be done before taking on that lifetime responsibility. While I believe Bobby sensed things between us were not the same after Deep Creek, neither of us ever spoke about it. We continued our weekly dates, until one evening after he had taken me home to Hickory. He leaned over to kiss me goodbye. "See you next week, Mary. I'll miss you every minute."

I had to do it now, but how could I? Bobby was a sweet guy and he would be hurt. We had enjoyed this evening together, as we had so many before. I breathed a prayer, "God give me strength."

My heart thumped so loudly, I wondered whether Bobby might hear it. "Uh," I swallowed hard, but the lump in my throat stayed. Suddenly, the words tumbled out. "Bobby, I need to talk with you about something really important. A couple months ago at revival meetings, I went forward to give my life completely to God. I asked Jesus to be my personal Savior. From here on, I want to do what pleases Him. I've come to realize I need to break my engagement with you."

"Mary! Oh, no!" The shock on his face was visible in the dim light. "Why? Don't you love me anymore? Mary. Mary, don't do this to me."

Shaken by his emotional outburst, I wavered momentarily

before going on. "Yes, Bobby, I still love you, but I also know I'm not ready for marriage. I need time and freedom to grow in understanding God's will for my life. I want to go away to Bible school at Eastern Mennonite and learn to know a larger circle of young people from other Virginia Conference churches."

"But I wouldn't keep you from going to Bible school. You know that," he insisted. "You could do whatever you wanted in your church."

We were both crying now and talking through tears. "Bobby, please, understand. It's more than Bible school and working in my home church at Mount Pleasant. I believe God may be calling me to full-time mission work. I do know, I want to teach children's Bible school somewhere besides here at home."

"Mary, I've got to know. Tell me, is there someone else?"

"No, Bobby," I spoke frankly. "At this time there isn't anyone else. That doesn't mean there won't be. I want to be free to date dedicated Christian boys in the future." Loosening the band on my wrist, I held the watch out. "Here, to be sure there's no misunderstanding, I'm giving back your engagement gift to me."

"No, Mary, no," Bobby said, shaking his head. "Even though our engagement is over, I want you to keep the watch as a token of my love for you."

We were quiet with our thoughts for several moments. Finally, Bobby broke the silence. "Well, I guess this time it really is goodbye," he said, cupping my face in his palms to tilt my chin upward. His lips tasted of salt, as he held me close for a moment and whispered, "I'll always love you, sweet Mary. Goodbye."

He turned and walked to his car. The engine cranked up, and I watched the taillights wink out the driveway, then disappear, as the car turned onto the highway.

Reality hit immediately. The impact was like a physical blow. Bobby was gone! Girl, are you out of your mind? Throwing away the promise of real happiness for a future of nothing! You could end up an old maid: no husband, no children–not even one. There go all your high-minded notions about a Christian home and family. I was helpless, trying to calm the storm raging in my mind. Finally, tired almost beyond endurance, I fell into bed, and eventually drifted off to fidgety, restless sleep.

Next morning, the struggle was on the moment I awakened. Something alive and vibrant inside me had been ripped away, leaving in place a painful, leaden weight. There wasn't a shred of the wonderful lightness I had felt at Deep Creek. If anything, the doubts had intensified. Had I really accomplished last evening what God wanted or merely succumbed to a foolish whim? Oh, why so many hard questions, when the Christian life promised answers? Maybe, I truly was happier before the revival service.

The turmoil raged, until I was driven to kneel by my bed. Opening my heart to the Lord, I prayed, "God you know my desire to serve you faithfully and to have your blessing on my life. This morning I again commit my will to yours. Give me strength for that purpose."

As I continued praying, peace slowly came to fill my anxious soul. The sense of loss still lingered-that needed time to heal. Future crises might test my faith, but God's overcoming grace would give me strength for the next hurdle. I was confident of that.

CHAPTER 10
A New Direction

THE SPIRITUAL experience at the Deep Creek revivals changed our lives forever. While before, having a good time had been one of our more important priorities, sister Fannie and I now set our course on being faithful followers of Jesus. It didn't mean we walked about sober-faced all day–we still enjoyed laughter. But undeniably, our interests had changed. Though, we had not altogether quit attending church activities, those with a strong spiritual theme had no longer held much appeal. But now, Fannie and I felt some urgency to attend Bible study and Literary Society meetings. We wanted those things that would further our Christian lives.

"Literary," as we called the biweekly Thursday evening meetings, was a combination business meeting, program, and social time afterward. While not a worship service, Literary had important benefits, nevertheless. Among other things, we learned correct parliamentary rules during the business session where Homer Wenger, a longtime Literary advocate, stressed *Robert's Rules of Order*. The programs, usually planned, but occasionally impromptu, included group and quartet singing, recitations, and skits. Literary gave us experience in speaking before an audience, and the informal social time helped draw us back into Mount Pleasant's larger youth group.

Earlier, stirred by Sunday school teacher Lydia Miller's stories and zeal for missions, I had dreamed of someday being a missionary. However, while going with Bobby, the vision had dimmed and almost disappeared. Now, once again, I felt God's Spirit prompting me to Christian service. With that I felt an urge for more Bible knowledge. Eastern Mennonite School–now Eastern Mennonite University–offered a six-weeks Bible course each winter. Known as "short term," classes began just after the New Year. I made plans to attend the 1947 session, without sister Fannie along. She had recently taken a job as driver for Ruth Thomas, who had an extensive newspaper route around old Norfolk and Princess Anne Counties.

In the months after my breaking up with Bobby C., I had several dates with fellows from the Mount Pleasant Church. While on a trip to Montana to visit my sister Lizzie, I had also met Morris K. with whom I began a friendly correspondence. Bobby, meanwhile, did not give up his efforts to win me back. Several times, he approached me with his persuasive best. "Mary, won't you reconsider? I really believe we could be happy together."

Though, I was becoming more certain with the passage of time, that my decision had been right; sometimes, a small "Well, maybe," crept in. Sister Fannie never failed to bolster my resolve during those times. "No, Mary. You can't let him persuade you. Don't even think of it," she would say.

About the time I was leaving for Bible school, one of Bobby's last attempts proved the most difficult. Aaron Mast, from Pennsylvania, had held a revival at Mount Pleasant, late December 1946. Bobby attended and responded to the evangelistic invitation one evening. This time he seemed certain, I would change my mind. "But Mary," he pleaded, in tears. "Last summer, you broke our engagement because I wasn't a Christian. Now, I've accepted Christ. Why won't you have me back?"

"Because, Bobby, I'm not ready for marriage," I replied, struggling to control my emotions. "I'm happy for you deciding to become a Christian. But at this point, I don't believe we are meant for each other."

Seeing his disappointment was painful. As I have said before, Bobby was a nice young man, and I had no desire to hurt him. The incident, among one of many over the years, added to my awareness that the Christian life is not a rose-strewn path. Rather, it is a hard, bumpy trail, marked by obstacles that often appear insurmountable. However, firsthand experience has taught me, that as we place our trust in God, He can take us over or around the most formidable barriers.

Though short term lasted only six weeks each year, the music study, church history, and soul-winning courses left a lasting impression for the two years I attended. I was awed by the instructors, particularly G. Irvin Lehman and Milton Brackbill. I saw them as great men of God and tried to absorb their every word. Brackbill's "Personal Soul-winning," course placed major emphasis on memorizing Scripture. Many of those Bible verses are still fresh in my memory, especially: "As it is written, There is none righteous, no, not one. . . ." (Romans 3:10); "That if thou shalt confess with thy mouth the Lord Jesus Christ, and shalt believe in thy heart that God hath raised him from the dead, thou shalt be saved. For with the heart man believeth unto righteousness; and with the mouth confession is made unto salvation." (Romans 10:9-10) King James Version.

In his Bible study course Brackbill strongly urged us to a daily regimen of Bible reading and prayer. "The reading and prayer need not be long," he'd say. "But read until God reveals a particular truth for your life that day."

Morris K., whom I had met the previous summer in Montana, was also at Eastern Mennonite that year, and the two of us dated several times during the six-weeks term. Though, Morris would not have been called handsome, I was attracted by his friendly personality and his fine Christian character–Morris would later serve many years as a pastor.

Campus rules were very strict. A formal date consisted of a few hours together in the lounge on Sunday afternoons. There, the dean of women kept a watchful eye from her nearby office for any misbehavior. Couples were not to hold hands or have any physical contact. Morris and I took long walks around the campus and ate meals together in the cafeteria. He was very interested in pursuing a serious relationship after short term ended. We wrote letters regularly for a time; however, I never felt God was leading us toward a life together.

Bible school helped keep me going the direction Fannie and I had chosen almost a year earlier. More participation in areawide church happenings had acquainted us with young people from the Warwick River Mennonite Church, forty miles from Mount Pleasant, on the north side of the James River. The six weeks at

Harrisonburg further broadened my horizon. Along with Bible knowledge and spiritual insight, I learned to know something about the larger Mennonite Church—a process that is still going on a half-century later.

My earlier heart cry for a Christian home and family had grown into a confidence that God would work His will for my life. Therefore, I felt no great impatience over not having a steady boyfriend. There were times, however, I found myself thinking about one particular Mount Pleasant fellow. We dated occasionally the summer of 1947, with the understanding that each was free to date others. Tall, handsome, with a shock of wavy hair, he should have caught any girl's eye. But he was so different from other young men I knew. While he would join in neighborhood baseball games, he drew back from the horseplay and laughter in which most young fellows usually engage. Behind blue-gray eyes lurked an earnest sincerity, well beyond his age. He would make a fine husband for someone one day. But, two years my junior at seventeen, he was too young for me. And besides, much as I wanted a Christian husband, maybe this fellow really was too serious for me. On the other hand, his spiritual discipline might be just what I needed as a growing Christian. At the time, I could not decide.

That year, 1947, Dad had a real estate office at Hickory, and I worked there part time as his secretary. I also worked two days a week for Clarence Byler, selling pork and poultry products at the Norfolk City Market. As the year wound down, I again made plans to attend the 1948 short term Bible school session. This time, sister Fannie joined me for the six weeks at Harrisonburg.

We stayed in the dorm during class week, but weekends were often spent in the Simon Tice home—Verna Mae Miller's parents and her younger twin sisters, Elva and Evelyn. Their mother, Naomi, was a gracious hostess and marvelous cook, seemingly always prepared for Sunday dinner guests. Among her favorite dishes of mine were creamed corn and Amish-fried potatoes—boiled potatoes, grated, fried, and seasoned with black pepper. The feast was never over until we had been plied with cake and several kinds of pie.

For all Naomi Tice's concern that we not leave hungry from her table, even more, she wanted us spiritually healthy. In a kind voice and sincere tone, she encouraged us to allow God to control our lives. Though never saying so, I'm sure Naomi sometimes had second thoughts about "those Troyer girls." Coming from a broken home and all; they spent so much time laughing and talking about boys!

Elva and Evelyn knew their way around the Harrisonburg Mennonite community, much larger than back home in southeast Virginia. The twins friendly warmth quickly drew Fannie and me into their circle of friends. Singing and playing music was a popular activity with this group. Musical instruments were acceptable here, and we would congregate in family members' homes for our musicfests. Needless to say, the atmosphere seemed more wholesome there, than some I had been accustomed to while going with Bobby. As I recall, we sometimes met at the home of Doyle M.'s aunt. Doyle M., a short-termer too, was also a fine guitarist. What else, but that I soon found myself attracted to him. By the end of Bible school, we had agreed to go steady, even though it meant maintaining the relationship by mail.

For all that I have described here, one might perceive we spent most of our free time in frivolous activity. We did not, I hasten to say. Fannie and I attended the revivals conducted by evangelist Nelson Kauffman. There we recommitted ourselves to Christ at an evening service and sought advice afterward where we might best serve in church work. Brother Kauffman directed Fannie to the Mennonite Children's Home at Kansas City, Missouri. About the same time, I received a letter from Brother Amos Wenger at Mount Pleasant, asking whether I would teach vacation Bible school in eastern Kentucky in May of that year.

Earlier, in a letter to one of my best friends, Leona Miller, I had expressed willingness to serve at Mount Pleasant, rather than seeking mission work away from home. That offer opened a door to many years of active participation in the life of the congregation. The opportunities to teach and be involved in other church ministries have brought a wealth of blessings beyond anything I could have imagined as a nineteen-year-old. However, for all the rewards that have come with serving in my home church, altogether, none can match what I gained from my voluntary service in late spring 1948.

Accepting the call to teach children's Bible school at Relief, Kentucky, brought a thrill of excitement, knowing I would be doing the Lord's work several hundred miles from home. Five of us would be going from the Mount Pleasant community: Rebecca Warfel, Amos Layman, James Bergey, Gordon Wenger, and I. James' assignment called for two weeks, while the rest of us would stay four weeks.

I did not think it significant at the time, that James Bergey was in the group. He was obviously no stranger. On a date several years before, I had considered him boyish and immature at fifteen. By 1947, as the young man I describe earlier in this chapter, James had begun to impress me with his Christian character and

Here I am (left) in the summer of 1948 with a group of students and fellow teachers Anna Hege and Amos Layman at the Bible school in Relief, Kentucky.

James (right) with Bible school students in Relief, Kentucky, in the summer of 1948.

thoughtful manners. Yet, I had not been convinced we were meant for each other. Now, a year later, James had a steady girlfriend, and I was corresponding with Doyle M.

Mahlon Horst and his wife, Leah, were the church mission workers at Relief, Kentucky. While genuinely pleased we had come to help with Bible school, Mahlon was emphatic about our behavior. "No courting. We don't want any hanky-panky going on" (a warning we laughed over long afterward). "We expect the girls to wear their cape dresses, when they go shopping in town. Just remember who you are," Mahlon reminded us.

After the first week Brother Otis Snead came from South Boston, Virginia, to hold a week-long revival at Crockett, four miles from the Horst home. A man of lively humor, Snead regaled us with his endless collection of funny stories. Learning that James and I had dated earlier, Snead began teasing us. I laughed at his urging that we "warm up the old soup again." That prospect wasn't likely, since we each had a special friend.

The trail to Crockett was all but impassable for a vehicle. That meant that we ladies made the trip on horseback, with the men afoot, leading our horses. Although, the evening services ended by dusk, it was always long past dark before we were back at the Horsts. The last evening of revival came, and afterward in the late twilight, we readied ourselves for the homeward trek. By chance or by design– I believe now the latter–James Bergey had my horse's rein in hand. Carefully, we picked our way along the rock-littered path, the saddle creaking beneath me, with James clutching the bridle.

Darkness came on, and the Kentucky hills almost disappeared, before a full moon etched the ragged peaks once more against the lighted sky. Down the hollow, a night bird called across the cool, quiet air; farther away, a barking dog bounced echoes round about the hills. Moonlight streaming through the spring leaves overhead dappled everything it touched: James, me, the horse, and the ground underfoot.

"Magical" describes that long-ago scene, but "magic" sometimes calls up visions of witches, goblins, and things evil. Remembering now, I believe "reverent" is a better word for what I felt along that mountain track. Long minutes passed with neither of us speaking. Was James absorbed in thought? I couldn't tell, until we stopped, abruptly. He turned to look up at me, the moonbeams casting an aura about his head and shoulders. "Mary," his voice came soft as a caress. "I'm wondering if you would go steady with me again, after we get back home again."

The other ladies and I rode horseback to the revival in Crockett, Kentucky.

The request didn't catch me totally off guard; though I wasn't ready for it just then. Admittedly, I had grown closer to James these past two weeks, but there was also my agreement with Doyle M. and James with his girlfriend at Mount Pleasant. I can't recall the thoughts running through my mind; however, knowing I didn't wish to make a hasty decision, I hesitantly replied, "Oh, maybe."

James' face plainly showed his disappointment. "Don't just say 'maybe,'" he said in a gentle, reproving tone. Turning away, he tugged on the bridle, and we were on our way, again in silence. Had he taken my reticence as simply being coy? I hoped not. For with all my indecision, I had begun to care about this young man's feelings. "But what about Doyle?" a voice within seemed to say. Oh, dear, why was everything so confusing? The only solution I could think was to pray about the matter overnight.

The following day passed all too soon, and time drew on for James and Brother Snead to leave for home in Virginia. Awkward as it was with everyone else around, I knew James wanted to talk with me alone before leaving. Finally, he and I went to a room for what was to be a private conversation–I learned later, Amos Layman eavesdropped outside the door all the while we were talking. "Mary, I just can't leave here without a clear answer to my question last night," James said, gazing into my eyes.

This time, the words came easily. "Yes, James. I'll go steady with you," I said.

He smiled, "That's what I hoped you'd say. Thank you, Mary." His courtesy came so naturally, I felt almost embarrassed. Polite terms would take some learning and getting used to on my part. "Thank you," "Please," and other such niceties were spoken to market customers, but seldom to a friend or family member.

During our further conversation, we agreed this time our relationship would be deeper and stronger than ever before. We also concluded that explanations to Doyle M. and James' girlfriend could be the most uncomfortable part of all this. Yet, despite my trepidation, almost instantly, I felt what we were doing was God's will. Confirmation arrived for me the next day in a letter from Doyle, who wrote that he believed it best for us to end our relationship. I read the words with immeasurable gratitude for the way God was directing my life.

Chapter 11
Your People Shall Be My People

> "... Where you go I will go, and where you stay I will stay. Your people will be my people and your God my God."
>
> (Ruth 1:16) New International Version.

RUTH, the Moabitess, spoke those memorable words to Naomi, her Jewish mother-in-law, more than three thousand years ago. In spring 1948, I made that same basic promise to James Bergey, the son of another Naomi–Naomi (Kemp) Bergey. While my "Yes, James. I'll go steady with you," was far less profound than Ruth's classic lines, I believe time would show that my intent was as sincere as hers. True, my situation could not match Ruth's. I wasn't leaving my community for a far-off land, nor giving up my religious faith. However, the "Your people will be my people" would turn into a struggle of many years.

But that would come later. There in Kentucky, everything shone gloriously beautiful midst the rush of excitement during the two weeks after James returned to Virginia. How quickly my former hesitance had become a growing assurance that I loved him! The daily letters we wrote to each other, no doubt, did much to encourage that belief. "Mary, I miss you so much and can't wait for you to come home," James wrote. "I love you, my jewel."

"Jewel," became his pet name for me. It thrilled me then, and since, when James has written or spoken the word. Though, he has used the endearment less frequently in later years, I have felt no less valued. Simply stated, when the children came, we wanted them to know us as "Mommy," and "Daddy," rather than by a nickname.

Courtship with James was nothing like my earlier relationship with Bobby C. Even during our engagement, I had never met Bobby's parents or members of his extended family. James immediately included me in his mother's Kemp-family gatherings. There was no more staying away from church services or hanging around the edge of youth activities. Rather than, "Let's go to a movie, Saturday night," James would ask, "Mary, will you come along to prayer meeting?" We attended the quarterly mission meetings that included the Mount Pleasant, Deep Creek, and Warwick River Mennonite congregations. We taught vacation Bible school at our home church and at Weeping Mary Baptist, the black church at nearby Fentress village.

James enjoyed exploring around Virginia and North Carolina. As a result, we sometimes spent holidays and Sunday afternoons on North Carolina's Outer Banks, stopping at the Wright Brothers Memorial, or hiking along the remote beach at Kitty Hawk.

Impressed though I was by James' mannerly behavior, I nevertheless, occasionally questioned whether I really deserved so much courtesy. "Please," and "Thank you," were new expressions for me in everyday conversation. But more remarkably, this fellow regularly opened the passenger-side car door and saw me seated before going around to take the wheel. Though James didn't engage in outright flattery, I think he was overly confident of my cooking skills. Evenings after he'd taken me home to Hickory, I often served a snack before he returned to Mount Pleasant. From the beginning, I wanted to be sure the food was to his liking. I asked on one occasion, "Tell me. what's your favorite pie and cake? Apple and peach pie? Oh, James, I want to learn to cook things exactly as you like them."

"Well, thank you, Mary," he said, smiling. "I know you're already a fine cook, and whatever you make will be good.' With that, he scraped a last bite from the saucer and changed the subject to one that made me uneasy. "I really must be going. Mother will be upset if I'm not home by eleven-thirty. She already thinks we're together too much as it is, you know."

It would be false to say that Naomi Bergey was altogether happy over her firstborn's choice of a serious girlfriend. Call it a woman's intuition, but I sensed that almost from the beginning. The knowledge left me with mixed feelings. While I didn't doubt James' love for me, my sometimes low self-confidence fell even lower, knowing his mother lacked enthusiasm for our courtship.

Was it because I was one of John and Dena Troyer's girls? Or, perhaps, that I didn't always obey the church dress code precisely? That thought struck me as ironic. I believed Bobby's family had considered me too plain. Now, I might not be conservative enough for James' family. Would I ever get it right? As our relationship progressed, I learned Naomi's stated misgivings were that nineteen was too young for James to be planning marriage.

Despite my personal uncertainty, James reassured me that he was pleased to be seen with me. His mother's family, the Kemps, were close-knit and held frequent family gatherings. Many of Naomi's relatives weren't Mennonite, and I felt shy and unrefined in their presence. Finding it difficult to join in conversation, in the beginning I remained silent more often than not. My lack of sociability did not discourage the Kemps. A number of them did their best to put me at ease. A few of the young married men seemed to delight in teasing about James and me getting married. My shyness, notwithstanding, I did not find the comments offensive, but rather took them as a sign of acceptance.

Meanwhile, James was also helping me get beyond my ingrained negative feelings. "You're beautiful, Mary," he would often say. "You look nice in that dress," and then, half-teasingly ask, "Do I look good enough to go out with you?"

Unaccustomed to compliments of that sort, I may have felt somewhat ill at ease; however, I quickly learned to appreciate them. As it turned out, the statements never grew old or meaningless from overuse. After forty-seven years of marriage the sincere warmth in James' voice, yet today, put "Mary, you're beautiful," among the most lovely words I shall ever hear.

While acceptance by the Kemp family and encouragement from James played important roles in my growing self-esteem, through Bible study and reading devotional material, I also learned to see myself as a unique part of God's creation. Not only had He made me, but with His everlasting love God had given me salvation through His son, Jesus Christ.

Today, a steady couple will often see each other daily, or at least talk together by phone. Back then, James and I were together on Sundays, and one or two weekday evenings–prayer meeting and a youth function. Phones in the 1940s had two main disadvantages. First, private lines were hardly available in rural areas. You shared a party line with three or four other customers. Consequently, no one could have a really "private" phone conversation. Also, most phone systems covered a relatively small area, and calls outside your neighborhood meant expensive long-distance charges. That was the situation when I was at home in Hickory, as well as the year, and more, I worked for two doctors' families: the Hills and Venners at Princess Anne. Though less than a dozen miles separated us in both instances, James and I wrote letters back and forth, two or three times weekly. For us, a ringing phone could not compare with the anticipation that came with the mailman's arrival. How delightful to get away by one's self and savor, "Darling," Sweetheart," and "I love you!" Sweet words, not unlike what countless lovers have always written, but these were uniquely ours, because of what James and I felt for one another.

As every couple discovers sooner or later, when two persons honestly strive to yield part of their individuality to one another, the result becomes a blend of romantic moments, serious-funny incidents, and sometimes painful differences. From those episodes one learns things about his or her partner, that may not get communicated in words. James and I found that to be our experience.

One of those insights came for me at a Saturday afternoon beach party. Until then, I had never seen James angry, and I doubt few, if any, Mount Pleasant young people had witnessed any display of temper from him. James Bergey was known as calm and unexcitable–a person who drew away from confrontation. That may have been partly the reason for what occurred there at Sandbridge beach. One of the young fellows, notoriously brash, made me the victim of a mean practical joke. Whether I screamed or cried, I don't recall, but I have never forgotten James' response.

He immediately rushed to my rescue. The prankster backed away laughing, assuming he had nothing to fear from mild-mannered James Bergey. Much to the tormentor's surprise—and probably everyone else—James charged in and began punching. As the fellow didn't attempt to defend himself, the incident was quickly over. Afterward, the wonderful feeling of being protected by James far outweighed my initial embarrassment at the prank.

We had gone steady only a few months, before the "M" word, marriage, cropped up in conversation. Our talk held none of the subtle, romantic hints in which some couples engage. James, the unsophisticated farm boy, and I, the ever-practical working girl, met the subject head-on. "What do you think, Mary, about us getting married?" he asked.

"Oh, I don't know. I couldn't marry anyone else, you know that. But, James, how could we possibly make a home, when we have nothing to begin with?" I replied. "No money and no place to live."

"Well, Dad told me lately, he'd give me a chance on the farm."

I murmured, "Oh, that could be nice," though, I wasn't sure what a "chance" meant. One thing I did know, James was only eighteen at the time, and I was certain, neither mother, Naomi, nor father, Titus, would look favorably on us getting married then. Like many Mennonite children raised on the family farm. James had never received wages for his work. Although, there were exceptions, many children worked for their parents until age twenty-one. Room and board were free, of course, but even clothes were bought and paid for by the parents.

There were several reasons involved with my concern over finances. For one, though my wages did not amount to very much at the time, that income would cease after we were married. A Mennonite wife's place then was in the home, and rarely would one be seen working at a day job. Along with that, I had also grown to appreciate living in Mom and Dad's new house at Hickory. No, they had not remarried, but Mom and Bud had lived only a year at Moyock, after Vernon Beard's death. Overwhelmed with loneliness, the two left the place off Puddin' Ridge and moved in with Dad, Fannie, and me. The move and the subsequent pooling of their funds to build a fine brick house, obviously, did nothing for our divorced parents' reputations. However, from all I could ever discern, the arrangement was nothing more than a business arrangement. Each had their own bedroom and kept their distance.

My divorced parents pooled their funds in 1946 and built this fine brick house at Hickory, Virginia.

Talk of marriage came up occasionally over the next year or so, but James and I didn't begin making serious plans. until early 1949. Meanwhile, I had been squirreling away money from my job at the Hills and Venners. Hard as I tried, savings from my weekly twenty dollars grew at a pitifully slow pace. Despite my love for James and the certainty that God intended for us to be together, the lack of a definite wage offer from his Dad continued to trouble me.

"James, just what does your Dad mean by 'a chance?'" I asked one evening, as we discussed plans for our future. "We have five hundred dollars and no car. What will we live on?"

Before James could answer, I went on. "You know, Brother Otis Snead offered you a good job at his orchard at South Boston. Wouldn't it be nice, James, for just the two of us to get away and be on our own?"

James tentatively agreed, "Well, yes, Snead's offer really did sound good. We'll consider that. But Mary, let's pray about it right now. Will you pray first?"

Oh, dear! Praying aloud in ideal circumstances was still a difficult task for me, and certainly now, with the tumult in my brain, I was not inclined to audibly speak to God. Nevertheless, I hid my discomfiture from James, as best I could, and struggled to be prayerful. The words came haltingly, "Dear God, we want you to help us as we think about getting married. We do want to live for you. Amen."

At that moment, I was keenly aware of my inexperience in praying. However, over time, I would learn prayer is like any other area of the Christian life. Through practice and discipline comes spiritual growth. I had to learn to forget about myself when coming into God's presence. As I prayed more devotedly, the better acquainted I became with Jesus, my Friend and Counselor. With that came the reality that prayer is the wonderful privilege of direct communication with God the Heavenly Father.

James and I became officially engaged sometime in late spring 1949. Neither of us can remember the exact time, since we had discussed marriage early in our courtship. As I pointed out earlier, the wearing of jewelry was forbidden for Mount Pleasant Church members then. Therefore, I didn't get or expect a diamond; instead, James presented me with a beautiful cedar chest, a gift that has become a family heirloom. I, in turn, gave him a four-by-five-inch black and white photo I had taken at a studio.

Mary (Troyer) Bergey at age eighteen in 1946.

As we made plans for a December wedding, the matter of where James would work and where we would live continued unresolved. Reflecting now, I realize James felt pulled in opposite directions. On the one hand, I wanted him to leave the farm, and, maybe, even move from our home community. On the other side was James' sense of duty to his parents-especially, to father Titus-and the family business.

Discussions on the subject usually left me less than satisfied. "Oh, Mary, Dad told me today if we stay and work on the farm, we can live in the old Bergey house rent-free," James said, one summer evening. Dad will ask the Brothers family to move, as soon as we give him a definite answer. He said they will help us with some furniture, give us ten dollars a week to buy groceries, and we can use their car. That way, we won't need to buy our own right away."

"Ten dollars a week!" I couldn't hide the dismay in my voice. "But James, how can we live on that?"

"Mary, I think we can." James said persuasively. "You can do our laundry at Mother's, and by helping with the garden, we can have vegetables to can and freeze. I'm sure we can put things in their freezer. I believe Dad will treat us right. Would you be willing to try it?"

"Oh, I hardly know what to say. I want to marry and be with you more than anything else. But I want us to be alone and have our own money, without having everything given to us. And what about our dream of doing mission work? If we get tied here on the farm, how could we ever answer a call from the mission board to serve in another area?"

"I know, Jewel, but Dad needs me here. Clyde will be going away to school. Byard helps Mother at the house and would only be able to do a few things around the barn. Without me, Dad won't be able to keep the dairy cows and do the farming. I do believe we must first be faithful where we are and wait for God to work things out for us."

Several years before, I had asked God for a Christian home and family. I had wondered sometimes since how He would answer that request. While I still had doubts about beginning married life on Bergey's Dairy Farm, I was convinced, nevertheless, that God had sent me this man, who would be a Christian husband and father if we were blessed with children. I said, "I want to be faithful too, and if that means staying here on the farm, then I am willing."

CHAPTER 12
As Long As We Both Shall Live

MIDSUMMER 1949 passed. Sister Fannie married Norman Teague in August. James and I set December 4 as our wedding date. This would not be a fancy affair. Financial constraints on my part, church rules, and our own desire to avoid worldly display, all decreed a simple ceremony. I bought silky-white rayon material and sewed it into a plain Mennonite cape dress-the pattern then worn by ladies of the congregation. We sent out invitations I had handwritten on note paper.

While not a first for Mount Pleasant, our wedding was, nevertheless, a break from the traditional exchange of vows at the bride's home. There were no decorations, flowers, or other ornamentation to indicate the 2:00 p.m. ceremony was any different from a Sunday morning church service. We had chosen James' brother Clyde and Laura Shaddinger to be our attendants-not until years later did the congregation find the standard wedding party acceptable, with bridesmaids, best men, and flower girl.

No one gave me away. With Clyde and Laura going first, James and I walked arm in arm down the aisle. I carried a Bible I had covered with leftover material from my wedding dress. We sat in the front pews, I on the ladies' side of the aisle and James on the men's, while James' grandfather, Clayton Bergey, preached the wedding sermon. Later described by a Kemp cousin as "long," the message extolled Christian marriage and the home. Grandpa Bergey also performed the ceremony.

Afterward, we and our guests went to Hickory, where Mom had prepared a reception of ice cream, cake, and punch. Although, James' grandmother, Malinda Kemp, recorded in her diary, "quite a lot of guests were there," I believe there were fewer than seventy-five.

Following the reception, we planned to drive eighty miles to a motel at Petersburg, Virginia. First, though, our wedding gifts were piled in the Bergey car and taken to Stanley and Maxine Warfel's

James and I were married on December 4, 1949.

Here James and I are flanked by our attendants, Laura Shaddinger (left) and James' brother Clyde (right).

apartment in the old Nash home along Mount Pleasant Road. The Warfels were spending a month with Maxine's relatives in Oregon. Stanley and Maxine had offered us temporary quarters, since Grandpa Bergey's house was still occupied by the Brothers family. Once the gifts were stowed away, I assumed, mistakenly, we'd be underway.

"Oh, yes," James said. "We must stop at home yet. The family wants to say 'Goodbye' before we leave."

We still needed to bid a formal farewell? It took a moment to sink in. They knew, full well, we were going for a five-day wedding trip, driving their car. Coming from my fractured-home background, this seemed like too much family togetherness. A quick hand wave, and "I'll be seeing you," were sentimental as anything I could have expected from my parents and siblings. In fact, almost certainly then, I would have recoiled if Mom or Dad had attempted to hug me.

That was not the way of my new husband's family. Today, I cherish the scene impressed in my memory of that evening; but I also recall a pang of jealousy, as James' parents and brothers, Clyde and Byard, gathered round to offer last-minute advice. "Drive carefully, now," his dad warned.

Mother Naomi kissed him warmly on the cheek, saying, "And don't forget, James, call us when you get to the motel tonight. We want to know you all are safe."

Much as we might desire otherwise, most of life's lessons are learned over months, years, and even decades. By bits and pieces, the Heavenly Father reveals a truth, hidden in the momentarily irksome, occasionally painful incident. The result of that gradual process is that we grow stronger in His grace, and into a better understanding of what God wants to teach us. Only long after our honeymoon did I begin to recognize my blessings from the attachment James had for his parents, brothers, and beyond to his Kemp relatives.

Finally, on our way that evening, we laughed over the instructions to call home. Our plan had been that no one, not even family members, should know where we would spend our wedding night. Since we have never lost our desire for certain privacies, I do not wish to share nuptial night details here. It is enough to say, James and I were gloriously happy, knowing we had kept ourselves for each other until God brought us together in holy matrimony.

For some, "honeymoon" calls up visions of Niagara Falls, an ocean cruise, or swaying palms on a tropical isle. Mainly because we lacked money for motels, but also in part for James' sociable nature, my honeymoon memories are of overnights spent in the homes of his Uncle Herm and Aunt Verna (Kemp) Bender, and former Eastern Mennonite High classmates. The Benders, a jolly middle-aged couple, lived at Springs, Pennsylvania, and doted on newlyweds. While their two-story farmhouse didn't offer a guest suite, Uncle Herm and Aunt Verna made certain a new couple found their stay unforgettable. James and I were ushered to the kitchen and their famous "honeymoon" chair. There, midst much laughter and joking, we were seated in the large overstuffed chair with James holding me.

Leaving the Benders, and on our way to Washington, D.C., we stayed one night with John and Mildred Landis at Chambersburg, Pennsylvania. After a day at the Washington Zoo, James and I drove to Harrisonburg, Virginia, to spend the last night of our trip with Isaac "Ike" and Mildred Risser.

Though our honeymoon may sound boring and unromantic, even for 1949, the story didn't end with the trip. Our visits with the Landises and Rissers brought lasting friendships, and we exchanged visits on a number of occasions. Today John and Mildred's daughter Cleta, husband Dennis, and son Shad live in our community and are members here at Mount Pleasant Mennonite Church. Mildred Risser's homemaking skills impressed me from the beginning. Her love of beauty was evident throughout their home—fine furniture, flowering plants, crocheted doilies, and tablecloths. As crocheting was one of my hobbies, I gleaned ideas from Mildred's handiwork. She also shared numerous of her mouthwatering recipes with me. Her raised doughnuts became longtime favorites at our house. James and I last visited the Rissers in 1994, at Hickory, North

Carolina, where Ike was pastor of the Mennonite Church.

Back home from our honeymoon, we settled temporarily into the Warfel apartment. I have never forgotten our first meal there. For all my cooking experience, I promptly lived up to the role of flustered bride by burning the potatoes. Embarrassed almost to tears, I apologized profusely, "Oh, James, I'm so sorry. I wanted this meal to be just right."

"It's okay, Mary. I know you're going to be a good cook." James did his best to soothe my injured pride. Like other incidents that seemed nerve-shattering at the time, this too became a source of humor for us later.

The month at Warfels flew by all too quickly. Stanley and Maxine arrived home from Oregon, and to my great disappointment the Brothers' family had not vacated the Grandpa Bergey house. Determined as I had been not to move in with James' parents, that was exactly what we did. Lest, after so many years I seem the ungrateful complainer, I must say those two weeks were not easy. Mother Naomi allowed me little opportunity to help around the house. Since January weather did not allow gardening or other outside work, I was like a caged bird. Most of my offers to help with housework were rebuffed. "No, no, Mary," Naomi insisted. "I'm doing laundry this morning, and you just put your clothes with our wash."

I had even more problems dealing with the constant displays of affection for James. The warmth of her hugs and kisses left me wondering if she did not know the Bible says in Genesis 2:24: "Therefore shall a man leave his father and his mother, and shall cleave unto his wife; and they shall be one flesh." King James Version.

Finally, six weeks after our wedding, we moved into the old Bergey house on Wenger Road, at the site where our son, Leonard, and daughter-in-law, Elsa, now live. Built by James' grandparents, Clayton and Amanda (Hendricks) Bergey, soon after their arrival at Mount Pleasant in 1910, the frame two-story must have been an imposing structure for the Mennonite community of that time. A large, windowed bay extended to the second-story roofline. The downstairs bay served as a foyer with an entrance from a roofed side porch. Inside, two doors off the foyer easily divided the living quarters into separate sections. As a result, the house was sometimes used as a two-family duplex in later years.

By 1950, the place was well past its prime. The exterior needed paint, and the bare wood floors inside were uneven, and doors didn't all latch properly. The outside

The first five years of our marriage we lived in the Bergey home built by James' grandfather in 1910.

walls weren't insulated, and the high-ceilinged rooms were uncomfortably cold during winter. In fact, there was no means for heating the four upstairs bedrooms. Despite all that, I loved the place, its roominess and the special character sometimes given off by an older, lived-in house—the sense of having weathered hard times and good; yet well capable of protecting its inhabitants from whatever storms might threaten. Though a later resident described the house as "spooky," the thought never occurred to me during the five years we lived there.

While I may have entertained thoughts about a touch of elegance here and there in order to quickly bring a nice, homey atmosphere to the old house, our meager income left nothing over for frills. The fact there were no window curtains didn't bother James in the least. When I first brought up the subject, his response was, "We just can't afford it now, Mary. Anyway, why do we even need curtains?"

Months passed before I had scrounged enough coins to buy inexpensive material, which I immediately began sewing into window drapes—something I believe nearly every woman considers a necessity. With Grandpa Clayton's permission, we took down a few well-worn furnishings from the third-floor attic. Titus and Naomi gave us a new blue dinette table with chrome legs and four matching chairs. They bought a new electric range, and we took their old kerosene cookstove. Almost everything could be aptly described as "Early Matrimonial," except the fine bedroom suite Dad presented as his wedding gift to us. He had originally bought the suite four years earlier to lure me and Fannie to come live with him at Hickory.

* * * *

Yes, early in our marriage I sometimes longed for nice furniture and kitchen appliances, and there were doubts about extended family relationships. However, beyond those earthly concerns grew a certain assurance of God working out His will for my life. He had blessed me with a loving husband, whose devotion to Christ and the church would become the solid footing for the Christian home I had pleaded for in 1946. With God's power and guidance, James and I would see our dream fulfilled.

Chapter 13
Joy and Heartbreak

FIFTY YEARS ago, few Mennonite ladies worked at day jobs after marriage. Unlike young couples today, weighing a wife's career against when to have children did not concern us. It was assumed babies would arrive soon enough if both partners were healthy. James and I wanted to begin a family immediately. Much to our disappointment, I did not become pregnant the first month, nor the second. Oh my, were we destined to be childless? Our fears are amusing now, but then, three months' waiting seemed to take forever.

By late April, early May 1950, my anxiety about becoming pregnant had given way to the misery of morning sickness. I fought nausea and loss of energy for six weeks during peak gardening time. Our share of vegetables came from the large garden at the Bergey farm. So I spent many days there helping Naomi and Grandma Kemp with the harvesting and processing. Grandpa Clayton, retired from the regular farm work, did most of the weeding and cultivating. That left us ladies with picking, hulling, canning, or freezing everything from peas, lima and snap beans to tomatoes and sweet corn. Long hours and hard work were nothing new, but dealing with listlessness midst the endless tasks was something to which I was not accustomed.

Nevertheless, feeling needed and able to contribute in the Titus Bergey home helped ease some of the tension I had always felt before in Naomi's presence. She was a marvelous cook, and that summer I learned to prepare many of James' favorite dishes. One was freshly killed chicken, cut up, browned in a skillet, then popped into a kettle with a tight lid and allowed to simmer for several hours. There was always dessert, and grapenut pudding was one of which James was particularly fond.

As I have said previously, times really were different then, particularly in the local Mennonite community. Six months into the pregnancy, I stopped attending Sunday services. By then, one was just "too big" to go about in public any more than was absolutely necessary. In fact, you didn't even mention your pregnancy to anyone except your husband and a few lady relatives and friends. Only after the baby's birth was the happy event shared outside this close-knit circle.

Along with that, perhaps, my own deep-felt need for privacy ran stronger than in most women. As the delivery drew nearer, I felt urged to tell James, "Darling, please, don't tell anyone, not even your Mom and Dad, when I begin labor. Okay?"

"Why not, Jewel?" he asked.

"Well, you know they would want to go along to the hospital, and I'm afraid I would be all but overwhelmed."

"All right, Mary. I guess we can keep it our secret," James agreed.

James' folks weren't the only persons keenly interested in exactly when I would be going to the hospital. By now, Ray and Nancy Hobbs were living upstairs from us in the Grandpa Bergey house. Questions and comments from Nancy told me, she too wished to be there when the moment arrived. As events occurred, no great lengths were needed to thwart the curious ones. We slipped out of the house around 2:00 a.m. on a Sunday morning-no one the wiser at such an early hour, I was sure.

Having awakened about midnight with lower back pains, I had waited only a few minutes before nudging James. "I believe it's time we head to Norfolk General," I said. The hospital was twenty miles away, and I wanted to be certain we got there before the baby came.

Not one to be hurried, James didn't feel my urgency. "Well, maybe we should wait until we're really sure." he said.

After an hour or more, the contractions had grown stronger and more frequent. We decided it was time to leave. However, before we had gone very far, the pains subsided. We drove around in the darkness, along deserted roads. There were no businesses open all night in 1950, but for one exception-Giant Open Air Market, in what is now Chesapeake, along Campostella Road, and also on our route to Norfolk General. We bought ice cream cones, ate, laughed and talked, before finally getting to the hospital about 5:30 a.m. Upon my being admitted, the nursing staff called our family doctor, who would do the delivery. After being told, "It will be awhile," James decided to go home to sleep. Except for the most determined, the small, spartan waiting room at old Norfolk General Hospital did not encourage long-term vigils. Lamaze classes were still in the distant future, and medical professionals, more or less, tolerated prospective fathers as a necessary inconvenience in the birthing process.

Our firstborn came into the world just before noon, November 26, 1950. Meanwhile, James had gone to Sunday services, without a word to anyone about what might be occurring at the hospital. After church, his phone call gave him the happy news about our baby boy. James then told Titus and Naomi they had become grandparents. We named our son James Harold II. As for my certainty that no one knew I had left home that morning, Ray and Nancy told us later, the rattle of a coat hanger dropped on the bare floor told them something was afoot in the other half of the old Bergey house.

Midst all our joy, the second day at the hospital brought on what is every mother's worst nightmare-switched babies. Though still groggy the day of the delivery, I was sure our baby had lots of thick, black hair. James had witnessed the same, just hours after the birth. To my surprise, the nurse brought me a blond-haired baby boy. When I voiced uncertainty, the nurse replied, "Oh, yes, he's yours. See here, his bracelet says 'B-E-R-G-E-Y.'"

Regardless of her most professional reassurance, the nurse hadn't convinced me. At the same time I was raising doubts, the other mother was adamantly proclaiming that she too had been given the wrong baby. She had been more wakeful than I and could readily identify her child. After tears from us, a lot of bustling about by hospital staff, and two doctors comparing what they knew, the little ones were reunited with their rightful mothers. Traumatic as the incident was, the hospital never gave us a satisfactory explanation for the mix-up.

Mothers with newborns were pampered back then. After four days, baby James Harold and I came home from the hospital.

The widow Lula Lehman came to the house daily for several weeks until I regained my strength. Lula helped me with baby Harold, the housework, and cooking. As a hardworking farmer, James was accustomed to hearty breakfasts and full course meals at midday and evening. With Lula's able help, we made certain that he never left the table hungry.

Busy as the next months were, I felt a growing contentment, watching little Harold thrive. His Daddy and I exulted over each stage of our son's development from first smile to sitting up to toddler. He showed special fondness for Titus and Naomi, who in turn, became the typical, doting grandparents to their first grandchild. I believed God was bringing about my prayer for a Christian home and family.

Harold was not yet a year old, when a visit to our family doctor confirmed what I all but knew to be true: our second child would be born the following June. We were excited, knowing Harold would soon have a baby brother or sister. As I recall, the pregnancy was mostly uneventful, except for my tumbling downstairs once and the usual bouts of morning sickness. However, on April 15, 1952, I felt the first pangs of what I knew should not be happening. The baby was not due for another ten weeks. Immediately, I was caught up in a two-sided struggle. On the one hand were the rapidly intensifying pains, while on the other, came a stifling fear over whether our child could survive a birth so premature.

The anesthesia then and the years since have dulled my memory of the exact details of our second son's birth, but I was well aware the next day that I hadn't yet seen the baby. When I enquired from my hospital bed, Dr. Harrington, a kindly, white-haired gentleman, hesitated. His blue eyes lost their twinkle and his voice became somber. "Mrs. Bergey, you have a tiny son, four pounds, eight ounces, with a head of thick dark hair. But I'm sorry to tell you, he's a blue baby and he'll need to be kept in the incubator and tube-fed until he gains some strength. He'll need to weigh five pounds before you take him home."

Stunning as they were, the doctor's words were only

beginning of things to come. Within days, we would learn John David had other serious medical problems-enlarged heart and liver and no vision in one eye. As often occurs shortly after birth, John David's weight dropped, but instead of rebounding after a few days like most babies, he continued to lose ounces.

The stress of it all left a dull, heavy ache deep inside me during all my waking moments. The burden became even greater when I was released and John David had to remain in the hospital. I so desperately wanted to nurse our tiny son, that I made daily trips to Norfolk General to deliver milk I had collected with the aid of a breast pump. For several days my efforts proved futile. At two weeks, our baby was down to three-and-a-half pounds.

Then came the frightening phone call from Norfolk General, "Come in at once. We've discovered your child has a strangulated hernia. He must have surgery immediately."

We rushed to the hospital and signed the necessary forms for the operation, but I felt in my heart the surgeon did not expect our son to survive. For days afterward, his life hung by a thread. The incision healed ever so slowly. Then with our hopes all but gone, he began to rally and put on weight bit by bit. Finally at five pounds, three ounces, and after six long weeks, we brought him home. I knew God had given us a miracle and fully believed He would heal John David completely.

How time and circumstances change us! Before, with Harold, I had wanted privacy and to be alone with my husband and firstborn. Now the community's loving response came as marvelous blessings. Many came to help and lend moral support. My sister, Edna, never failed when I most needed her. Roberta Buckwalter and her daughter, Shirley, were only the first among neighbors and friends who came to visit. Never had the simple phrase, "We're praying for you and your family," carried so much meaning. One of the first days after we brought John David home, two of my best friends, Maxine Warfel and Martha Hochstetler, came to visit. Their cheerful conversation and genuine interest lifted my sagging spirits. "Oh. he's so adorable. Look at that head full of hair. Here, let me hold the little fellow."

John David's growth, admittedly, was slower than that of other babies; nevertheless, we felt some encouragement over his early progress. He smiled at three months, laughed aloud at five months, and reached for his bottle at eight months. After an initial growth spurt, he weighed nine pounds, three ounces, by the end of six months, but only gained three pounds during the next year. While we were often anxious over his small size and frail condition, taking John David out in public was especially difficult

My mother holds John David in the living room of our first home.

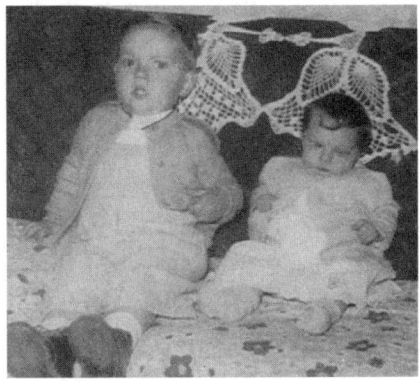

Our sons James Harold and John David in 1953.

for me. People stared, whispered behind their hands, and now and again, one would ask, "What is the matter with your child? How old is he? Fourteen months? He's so small."

All of that, however, was nothing compared with the frightening episodes that began in October 1952, when John David, six months old, began having fainting spells. To me, they seemed like heart attacks. He would cry softly, his little face wreathed in pain, and then lapse into brief periods of unconsciousness. I would hold him gently all the while, trying to keep him comfortable as I could.

* * * *

Chronic health problems take their toll on a family, especially, when small children are involved. In most instances the mother is the primary caregiver, and it can be very difficult not to become totally absorbed with the ailing child. Sometimes, I found myself in that dilemma, and then trying to find more time for husband James and two-year-old Harold. One of those especially demanding times came when John David was eleven months old. A fainting spell, combined with a bad cold and a temperature of 104 degrees signaled the onset of measles. He remained very sick for days, some which were given altogether to his care.

Though Harold was too young to understand much of what was taking place, I wondered sometimes what might be going on in his little mind. An incident just before Easter reminded me that healthy children also need and appreciate a parent's undivided attention. John David had improved somewhat, and I took time to boil and dye eggs. Harold watched, wide-eyed, as the brightly colored eggs came out of the liquid. With just the two of us involved, he apparently saw the project as something I was doing especially for him. To this day, I remember his childish delight and the warmth of his, "Oh, thank you, Mother!"

From John David's birth, we had prayed God for a miracle of healing for him. We believed, despite his rather serious physical problems, he could grow up a healthy child. While we knew God could do this in an instant, we also trusted Him to work through the medical profession. As spring 1953 waned and John David's overall condition showed no improvement, we began seeking help outside our local area–Norfolk's Children's Hospital of the King's Daughters was still several years in the future. The Medical College of Virginia Hospital in Richmond seemed to offer the best hope.

I made the appointment for James and me to take John David there on Monday, June 15. While I knew he would need to remain at MCV for observation, at least a day or two, it was, nevertheless, a difficult trip back home to Mount Pleasant, without our baby. Next day, the empty place in my heart seemed much larger than John David's mere physical absence from the house. The day following, Wednesday, and unable to wait any longer, I phoned the Medical College of Virginia. The voice on the line was soothing, but noncommittal, "Yes, Mrs. Bergey, your son is fine. No, no, we really don't have any more information at this moment. As you must know, these tests do take time. Possibly, we'll have some results tomorrow."

On Thursday, the message from MCV was, "No, John David is not yet ready to be released." However, a day later during a phone conversation, Dr. Painter had promising news. "We believe surgery can benefit your son. Everything points toward that at this time." With hopes raised, James and I drove to Richmond on Sunday forenoon. How wonderful to hold John David in my arms, after a week's separation! The little fellow smiled and cooed, happy to again be with his Mommy and Daddy.

We were told by the nursing staff, the head surgeon needed to speak with us before John David could be released. The doctor, an older man, was detached and very professional. I struggled to understand what he was saying, but the longer he spoke the farther his voice seemed to fade off. "I'm sorry, Mister and Mrs. Bergey, but surgery will not help your son; there is nothing more we can do for him here."

James and I asked a brief question or two. The doctor's blunt answer convinced me, I was surely losing my hearing now, here at the end. "We believe your child may have a maximum of six months to live."

I wanted to scream, "No! No! Not John David, our precious baby," but didn't speak a word. Forty years ago, people displayed far less emotion in public, and Mennonites in particular, seldom expressed their true feelings before the world's prying eyes.

The next days were dreadful. Coping with the utter finality of Medical College of Virginia's prognosis for John David left me drained of energy. But, I could not let fear about the future gain control. There were too many things to be done in the present: meals cooked, clothes washed, children cared for, and the countless other tasks that fill a farmwife's days. My diary pages remind me, on various days, "I made blackberry jelly, sewed curtains, painted a room and mowed lawn," and on a Sunday: "We had a lot of company." Tired as I often was, the work was also a blessing. It helped take the edge off, "Your child has six months to live,"–dreadful words, clouding the sunshine from most of my waking hours. But, thank God, there was one bright spot.

We were not alone then, nor since, when our family has faced a crisis. Compared to Mom's lonely, overwhelming grief at Vernon Beard's death, there is no denying the burdens have been lightened by the presence and support of relatives and friends. Several persons provided help as the summer wore on. Roberta Buckwalter looked after Harold and John David, while I taught two weeks of vacation Bible school at Mount Pleasant. Mother Naomi kept the boys occasionally on Sunday afternoon when James and I were involved in a church event.

By early autumn, severe bouts of morning sickness and an unrelenting backache left me almost helpless. Marian Wenger came to do the laundry, and Roberta Buckwalter ironed for us. Mother Naomi cooked our noon meals several days. With the doctor's confirmation of my third pregnancy, I also learned I would need three weeks of daily back treatments with Dr. Wright in Norfolk.

The second week of those scheduled treatments began Monday, October 12, 1953. I drove our car, and took the boys along. John David rode quietly in his carry seat, while Harold kept up a three-year-old's normal chatter. "Look, Mother. What's that? When will we be there?" Once at the doctor's office, the nurse brought out a few small toys to entertain the boys, though I could usually depend on them to wait quietly while I was being treated.

The following day, Harold was up from his afternoon nap, and I had begun preparing food for the evening meal when John David began to cry. Going to pick him up, I saw at once he was suffering intense pain. Since we didn't have a phone, I quickly sent Harold, almost three, across the road to the Buckwalters, for Roberta to summon James from the farm, a half-mile away. Never in my life have I been so frightened and alone, as in those next dreadful moments. Helpless, I held John David to me and felt his life fading with each shortened breath. Then, of a sudden, his little body grew still, and I knew our darling was gone. Grief came like an overwhelming flood. Scarcely aware that Roberta and other neighbors were arriving, I sat in numbed silence while every fiber of my being cried, "Why, God? Why? Why does it have to be this way?"

Until James arrived shortly afterward, I did not move from my chair. His soft touch against my shoulder and the gentle sadness in his voice brought me back to my surroundings. "Mary, wouldn't it be better if you put John David down on the sofa for now?"

I agreed to that. We then phoned Dr. Harrington, who came to officially confirm our son's death. The doctor advised us to contact Francis Gay Funeral Home to arrange for the burial. Traumatic as this day had already been, nothing would compare with the wrenching agony when the undertaker laid the small body in a padded suitcase, to carry him away.

Only parents who have experienced it can know how deeply hurt James and I were over the death of our child. In the beginning, we went about in a daze. But there was also a sharpened awareness that left unforgettable memories: John David in his little blue casket on a stand in the living room the night before the funeral; the Friday afternoon service at Mount Pleasant Church, October 16, with hymns that included "My Jesus as Thou Wilt" and "Go to Thy Rest Dear Child." Throughout the funeral and several weeks beyond, friends and family members comforted us with their presence and expressions of sympathy. They brought meals and took care of the housework at a time when our young family was struggling with grief over John David's death and the added stress of my back problems.

Much as that circle of friends meant, I was also blessed with two of the greatest assets anyone can have through hard times–a wonderful mate and Christian faith. While James, always busy with farm chores, could not help with housework, as some husbands do today, his gentle patience and moral support remained constant. Along with all that, James did not miss a day telling me: "I love you, Mary,"–precious words for a wife in any circumstance, and especially so when trials come. Finally, though my trust sometimes wavered, my greatest comfort came from believing God would work out His will for us. Praying together with James and regular Bible study helped keep me focused on Jesus Christ.

CHAPTER 14
Pursuing the Goal

"Children are a gift from God; they are his reward."
(Psalm 127:3) The Living Bible.

WHAT a blessed Scriptural truth! With the approach of spring 1954, I was in the final months of my third pregnancy. Having been through this twice before, I struggled with opposing emotions. The thought of cuddling a new baby brought a momentary thrill of excitement, only to be replaced by apprehension. For all John David's short life had brought us, I was concerned that this child might also be born with serious medical problems. Much to our delight, we had a robust son born May 13, 1954. James and I named him Leonard, and praised God for giving us a healthy child.

Our family increased rapidly after that: Kathy was born in 1955; Floyd, 1956; Daniel, 1959; and Joy, 1961–Lynn, our seventh surviving child was born in 1970. Needless to say, with six children and the oldest not yet twelve, we were busy parents, James with the farm work, and I, as a young housewife and mother. In 1954, we built our present home, with the Bergey clan doing most of the construction. Often, by day's end, I was bone tired; nevertheless, I did not begrudge the endless tasks that are part of a growing family. Life has richness and depth where God and love are present.

Although my interest in church-related activities had increased greatly after the Deep Creek revivals in 1946, courtship and marriage to James strengthened the desire to be a faithful follower of Jesus. An important part of that walk meant regular attendance at Sunday school, preaching services, and Wednesday evening prayer meeting. While, for custom's sake, I had stayed home from church during the last months of my early pregnancies, that changed at once after the baby's birth. As I recall, Harold's first outing was a midweek prayer meeting at Mount Pleasant Church. Our commitment to attend scheduled services remained firm during our children's growing years. In fact, Harold recently recalled that he and his siblings were among the few adolescents attending the Wednesday evening meetings.

The influence of church showed itself even in the children's games. They would hold pretend services, with Kathy and Joy leading songs and the boys taking turns preaching. Daniel, especially, relished his role as minister. "Open your Bible to the Psalms," he would solemnly pronounce, and in the next breath make a funny comment that sent his audience into gales of laughter. Over all, though, Daniel seemed to understand the weight of church responsibilities. Six years old, when James was ordained deacon, Daniel asked in sober tones, "Daddy, are we all deacons now?"

What was obviously then child's play has grown into reality for Harold since 1991, when he was installed as pastor here at Mount Pleasant Mennonite Church, Chesapeake, Virginia.

Encouraged strongly by church leaders to instill Biblical principles into our children, James and I attempted to teach them by both word and example. Back then, we didn't own a television set, and evenings before bedtime, we read to them-Bible stories, Laura Ingalls Wilder's books, *Winnie the Pooh, A Hive of Busy Bees*, among many others. I continued reading until a child reached the age where he or she no longer took time to listen. Nightly prayers were a bedtime ritual with each one until age twelve or thirteen.

* * * *

Of all the sorrowful events our family faced through the years, none came with the awful suddenness, as the one that struck in the summer of 1961. Seven years earlier, James' next younger brother, Clyde, had married Helen Dickerson. Clyde, a six-footer, dark-haired and handsome, had a lively humor that overflowed easily into rippling laughter. He, James, and father Titus had formed a partnership several years before with the farm and dairy operation (Byard, the third brother, still in school, chose not to join the company). Now, in 1961, Clyde and Helen had five small children, including five-year-old twins, Ray and Roy.

Helen's extended family–parents, Roy Sr. and Sylvia Dickerson–held an evening picnic at Munden Point, in Virginia Beach, July 27. Clyde's family was among the first to arrive. Having brought along his small outboard motorboat, Clyde put the twins and his brother-in-law, ten-year-old Donnie Dickerson, into the boat, then climbed in after for a pleasant ride along Currituck Sound's north edge. The water off Munden Point is quite shallow at low tide, wading depth, even hundreds of feet offshore. After a bit, the boat was stopped, and Clyde and Donnie could be seen splashing about in the water. Since no one heard shouts for help, it was assumed Clyde and Donnie were taking a dip.

Suddenly, however, the observers on shore were shaken, when the pair disappeared from view. and the twins were left alone in the boat. Donnie's oldest brother, Walter "Doc" Dickerson, recently

Our extended family, before Clyde's death, included back row, left to right, Titus, Byard, James holding Kathy, and Clyde holding one of the twins. In front are James Harold, Naomi (Mother Bergey), Leonard, Grandma Malinda Kemp, myself holding Floyd, and Helen (Clyde's wife) holding the other twin.

recalled his own involvement in the tragedy. "The boat was probably four hundred yards out. I waded and swam across the deep holes. The little boys were in the boat crying, but there was no sign of Clyde or Donnie. I got into the boat, and then couldn't get the motor started." The remembered pain showed clearly on Doc's face as he added, "I ended up rowing all the way back."

Helen called us with the heartbreaking news. "Please, come at once," she sobbed. We rushed to the scene, twenty-odd miles away, where police and rescue crews were already searching. They would find Donnie's body that evening yet before full dark; however, not until the following midday was Clyde's body retrieved, after being located by a spotter plane. The twins, Ray and Roy, were able to give a few details as to what had occurred. Donnie had apparently fallen overboard, and Clyde, not a good swimmer, was caught up in the momentary panic to rescue his young brother-in-law.

Clyde Bergey, James' younger brother, died in 1961.

The utter despair brought on by such tragedies can leave one feeling helpless and uncertain. I believe that is how both the Bergey and Dickerson families felt for quite a time afterward. We had lost a beloved brother, Christian son, husband, father, and business partner. He would never again share with us his calm influence and easy laughter. Even now, I can hear his pleasant compliments, when I wore a new dress: "Mary, you look nice today."

Hard as the blow was for us, it struck the Dickersons even harder. Donnie–the youngest of Roy and Sylvia's children–and Clyde's deaths came only three weeks after father Roy Sr.'s funeral. And seven months earlier, another son, Lloyd, had perished in an accidental drowning at Sarasota, Florida.

The alternative to feeling hostile and blaming God for such circumstances seems to lie somewhere in the context of Doc

Dickerson's statement, as he remembered the sad occurrence: "Yes, it was terrible, but afterwards, you finally just have to pick up and go on."

* * * *

Praise the Lord for the positive changes that take place, as we allow Him to mold us in His likeness. One of those blessed transformations occurred in my feelings towards James' mother, Naomi. As our family grew, I became increasingly dependent on "Grandma" during crises. By that, I am not forgetting how much I turned to my sister Edna, along with other friends who have been wonderfully supportive, at times of my or the children's ill health.

My own mother, Dena, who visited occasionally, was far less involved with our family for several reasons. She had a full-time job; lived outside the community, and had no connection with Mount Pleasant Church life. However, I must note that Mom, while alienated from her Amish and Mennonite connections, had joined Indian Creek Baptist Church, near Hickory, Virginia, and was a faithful member there for many years. In fact, around 1961–62, our family attended a Sunday service at the church, where Mom was honored as "Mother of the Year." After a disabling stroke in 1963, she lived most of her remaining five years with sister Edna's family.

Dad, John Troyer, had moved from Hickory in 1952, married a German-born wife, and lived in Louisa County, Virginia, until his death in 1969.

It seemed sometimes, one crisis followed another in our young family. A particularly trying one occurred when Kathy, six-weeks-old, was rushed to Norfolk General for an emergency hernia surgery. Mingled with the memories is the unforgettable moment my baby awakened from the anesthesia with several tubes attached to her tiny body. Obviously in pain, her faint mewling cry–like a wee kitten's–would have torn any mother's heartstrings. Since Kathy was nursing at the time, I felt compelled to remain at the hospital day and night, however, there was also the hovering concern about what was happening at home with my husband and two small sons. The load was eased somewhat with the knowledge they were well-cared for by mother and grandma Naomi.

Over the years, I developed a deep love and appreciation for Mother Bergey—the name by which family and friends knew her. The strong bond she had to her immediate and extended families exists yet today. James and I still occasionally meet with his Kemp cousins—Naomi's nephews and nieces-for warm social times. At her death in 1982, I realized I had lost far more than my mother-in-law. Naomi (Kemp) Bergey was also my dear intimate friend, who had modeled the role of Christian wife and mother more than any other person in my life.

Nine and one-half years after John David's death on February 3, 1963, we had a stillborn son, following a full-term pregnancy. Though, I was told the baby had thick, dark hair and a beautiful face, I was not allowed to see him. For with his lovely features, the baby also had serious physical deformities, including intestines formed outside his body. Our doctor thought it would be too traumatic for me to see all this. Long afterward, I struggled to get past my anger and grief for having been denied the privilege of viewing my baby. Despite the emotional distress I might have experienced, I, nevertheless, knew this child had been part of me for the preceding nine months.

Only a few weeks after that, I became seriously ill with nephritis, a kidney ailment, and again spent two weeks in the hospital. I was told during my hospital stay never to become pregnant again; to do so, could very well prove fatal. James and I chose for me not to have surgery then to prevent another pregnancy.

Eight years went by. I had reason to believe I was in menopause, then abruptly discovered I was pregnant again. The news frightened me, needless to say. The earlier warning loomed large now, as I worried over what would happen with James and the children should I not survive the pregnancy. Knowing our pastor Philip Miller's wife, Verna Mae, would listen, I went to her with my concerns. The sincerity of Verna Mae's faith and words of reassurance were just what I needed. "Mary," she said, "We need to trust. We need to trust the Lord with the confidence of knowing our lives are in His hand. Remember what Romans 8:28 says: 'And we know that all things work together for good to them that love God, to them who are called according to his purpose.'"

There were no unusual complications during the nine months of pregnancy; however, I began to spot as time for the delivery neared. Dr. Harrington ordered me hospitalized for observation. Matters grew worse when I began hemorrhaging as the night progressed. Meanwhile, Verna Mae, unaware of what was occurring, awakened and heard God calling her to pray. She obeyed and spent several hours praying specifically for me.

Next morning, after the doctor determined a slowing of the baby's heartbeat, I was rushed to surgery and delivered a son by Cesarean section. We named him Lynn and thanked God for a healthy child and sparing my life, as well. Lynn's birth, however, ended my childbearing years at age forty-two. Before the surgery, James and I had signed the necessary forms for a tubal ligation.

Scary as the events leading to Lynn's birth had been, everyone rejoiced in our "miracle" child. His older siblings showered this late-born brother with their love and attention. He responded, early on, with a sunny disposition that brought us much happiness midst a decade of struggle and adjustment in our family.

* * * *

While life's sudden traumatic events bring raw, exquisite wounds, once past, we try to find closure and healing and move on from those painful incidents. In our experience, the long-term burdens are the most troublesome and can all but absorb a family's emotional reserves. For us, me in particular, having three of our children diagnosed with diabetes has been a very difficult ordeal.

The year, 1969, I was pregnant with Lynn, Kathy, fourteen, developed symptoms we didn't understand in the beginning. A sore on her back refused to heal; that, along with frequent nighttime trips to the bathroom, convinced us to seek medical attention. At the doctor's office, we were told Kathy was diabetic and would need to be hospitalized several days in order to stabilize her blood sugar and would also be taught to administer her own insulin.

Managing diabetes then was far more troublesome than today. There were no home blood glucose testing monitors in the early 1970s. Too often, regulating insulin dosage turned into what seemed a hit or miss exercise. The patient at home had only a urine test tape that indicated when relatively high blood sugar levels were being thrown off by the kidneys. Determining insulin need from the test tape was, as someone aptly described, "like trying to hit a baseball by seeing its shadow."

I directed much attention to Kathy's care. There were regular visits to the doctor and trying to be sure she kept to a proper diet. Unfortunately, because parents are human, we often come up short while dealing with a long-term crisis. There were times I felt remorse for neglecting the other children's emotional needs. Joy, only eight when Kathy's diabetes was diagnosed, seemed compelled to take on the housework and chores her older sister was unable to do. Between age nine and fourteen, she missed school numerous times to help out at home, saying on one occasion, "I wish I had diabetes, so I could get the attention Kathy does."

The words would become a dreadful omen. In 1975, Joy developed similar symptoms to Kathy's six years earlier. I have not forgotten the visit to the doctor's office and the same grim word from before–*diabetes!* Once outside in the parking lot, Joy and I stood by the car, held each other, and wept. It seemed unfair that she too, at fourteen, should be struck with this burdensome illness; and then in 1980, son Harold, age thirty, would learn that he was also dealing with the same malady.

Indeed, those years tried my spiritual resolve. Though I didn't lose faith, there were times when God seemed far away. However, through the darkest times, I clung to His Word. I kept in my recipe drawer a devotional booklet from which I could daily draw comfort and hope. Among the Scriptural promises I claimed Psalm 46:1: "God is our refuge and strength, a very present help in trouble."

Those words became reality, as I struggled toward a deeper trust in God's will. That and James' steady support helped carry me over the roughest spots. With each passing year, I became more confident my decision to marry James Bergey had been the right one. The certainty of that was reinforced ten or twelve years into our marriage.

One day, while out shopping with the children, I ran into Bobby C. We enjoyed several minutes of friendly conversation. He was still involved with music, and told me, rather nonchalantly, he'd been playing at nightclubs around Norfolk and Virginia Beach in recent years. Covering my astonishment as best I could, my thoughts ran back to the time we had dreamed of a musical career together. I recalled we were going to limit our performances to clean, family-centered settings and had vowed to stay away from dance halls and nightspots. So much for my girlish ideals and innocence! If there had ever been any doubts in my mind before, they were gone forever after that encounter.

I went home, thanked the Lord then, and many times since, for having given me courage and strength to stand by that painful choice of breaking our engagement on a summer's night in 1946. God, ever faithful, has since blessed me with a husband and children who love Him. I trust that by His grace, we have striven, imperfectly at best, to exemplify what a Christian family ought to be.

Having described a number of unfortunate incidents here doesn't mean ours was a cheerless existence. Rather, when asked recently about enjoyable experiences during their growing-up years, the children remembered visits with friends in Shenandoah Valley, Virginia, and Pennsylvania, and sightseeing trips to Michigan and Great Smoky Mountain National Park, among others. Son Floyd recalled his delight in learning to know new friends on those excursions. Even on our camping trip to the Smokies, we wound up at the Ed Godshall home in Hickory, North Carolina. There were also occasional Chesapeake Bay and ocean fishing trips from North Carolina's Outer Banks with James and the boys.

Unusual as it may sound in today's entertainment-driven society, the children's fondest memories seem to center around events close to home: wiener roasts, picnics, and homemade ice cream with relatives and neighbors down in the woods or at Sandbridge in Virginia Beach. Harold and Floyd both expressly mentioned our custom of hosting guests. "It was always exciting to have missionaries at our house," Floyd said. "To hear them tell stories about faraway places and people."

Harold added, "The hospitality was a major influence in my childhood and youth. I think every evangelist who preached at Mount Pleasant also visited in our home—George R. Brunk II, Myron Augsburger, Joe Esh. . . ."

Harold went on to recall an incident that involved the late Amos D. Wenger, Mount Pleasant pastor and longtime principal at Mount Pleasant Christian School. His sister, Rhoda Wenger, was home on furlough from mission service in East Africa. "The light teasing and banter that went on between Brother Wenger and his sister gave me a new perspective of this man, whom I'd always seen before as an authority figure," Harold said. "Rhoda was telling snake stories-several that involved her own narrow escapes. 'Well, I think I'd carry a gun,'" Amos said.

"Whereupon Rhoda replied, 'And a fine missionary you'd be, walking around Tanzania with a gun.'"

Just as in my own childhood, when daily work sometimes became a recreational activity, our son Leonard remembered the pleasure that went with getting the sweet corn harvest in for our family freezers. "It was fun to have everyone together, Grandpa and Grandma, Clyde's family, and us. After morning chores, the older men and boys would go to the field and pull off the ears. They'd pull the wagon into the shade, and we'd gather 'round and begin husking. There would be talking and laughter. Later, Grandpa would blanch the corn over at the dairy plant. You could eat as much blanched corn as you were able. The big meal at noon or in the evening was always something to remember."

"Doing corn" really was a special event for all of us. However, the day began at 5:00 a.m. for the Bergey ladies, rather than after morning chores, as Leonard remembered. There was food to be prepared for the hungry crowd of workers. We boiled and diced potatoes for salad, fried hamburger for Sloppy Joe's, baked sandwich rolls, and fresh peach pies. On one occasion, Grandpa–James' dad, Titus-dropped a peach pie, going out our back door. Seeing his contrition over the mishap left me feeling sorrier for him, than for the loss of the pie.

We usually planned sweet corn processing for Thursday– when the dairy plant was shut down. That not only allowed the men to help, but also gave us access to the plant's live steam hose for steaming the corn the needed seven minutes. The work flowed in a steady rhythm–James and a few helpers bringing the corn from the field; several adult volunteers and the older children husking the ears and removing the silks; Grandpa running the steam and popping the corn into ice water to cool it. Then it was time for us ladies to get busy cutting the tender kernels from the cobs.

Since we enjoyed sharing our harvest with people in the community, there were often other than just the Bergey families involved in the work. After a long, full day there would be one hundred or more quarts of prepared fresh corn in plastic bags and containers, ready for the freezer.

Like so many other changes that time brings, we no longer have "corn days." For one thing the dairy plant is in operation every day, and besides, our family members concluded some years ago, all the effort of putting up corn was insufficient for the end result.

* * * *

Through all the pressures of farming, business, and raising a family, James and I always found time for church responsibilities. His positions have included Sunday school teacher, superintendent, church treasurer, ordained deacon (June 1965), and licensed pastor at Deep Creek Mennonite, 1984–90. James also served twenty-four years, 1960–84, on Mount Pleasant's jail ministry team. During some of those years, our sons helped their Dad prepare Bible study correspondence lessons for the inmates, and James and I would afterward grade the material.

I taught many vacation Bible school and Sunday school classes for ages early childhood, through youth and older ladies. Along with that were stints on the Food Committee and several terms as president of our local Women's Missionary Service Commission. Along with serving in our home congregation, we always kept an active interest and vision for foreign missions. James and I attended churchwide missions meetings, and he served twelve years as a member of the Virginia Mennonite Conference Missions Board. On the practical side, we took advantage of many opportunities to host visiting missionaries and their families–some for only a meal, and others for several days at a time.

If the children have learned anything by our example. God alone is worthy of praise. Nevertheless, we are blessed to see them and their spouses serving the Lord, each in his or her own special place. All have participated in teaching Bible school or some other form of church-related service, at one time or another. Among the longer term stints have been Harold's pastorate at Mount Pleasant Mennonite Church, and Kathy's principalship at Mount Pleasant Christian School since 1989.

Harold and his wife, Rose, have four children, all teenagers: Philip, Jesse, Sara Joy, and Jamie. Kathy has three children: Christa, Matthew, and Jae.

Leonard and his wife, Elsa, have one son, David. Now general manager of Bergey's Dairy, Leonard spent two years with an agricultural project in Ghana, Africa, during the 1970s. Floyd, our farm and herd manager, is deeply committed to being a godly husband and father to his growing family. He and his wife, Debbie, are parents to Laura Joy, Erin, Joel, and Katie.

Daniel, who formerly owned an auto repair business, moved his family to Harrisonburg, Virginia, where he studied three years at Cornerstone Bible College in preparation for full-time church ministry. Daniel and his wife, Dorcas, have three daughters: Jennifer, April, and Rachel.

Joy works as part-time secretary for Bergey's Dairy, and her husband, Mike Morris, serves as route manager for the company. Earlier, Joy attended Columbia (South Carolina) Bible College and today God is using her in a unique way to minister daily in the lives of those around her.

Our youngest, Lynn, spent two years in Youth Evangelism Service, and has since chosen aviation as a career. He is currently licensed to fly commercial multiengine aircraft and holds a flight instructor's license, as well. Lynn lives with his wife, Lori, in Lancaster, Pennsylvania.

James and I are happy for each one's individual achievements, but our greater joy is in their growing Christian commitment. If anything can match that blessing, it is our grandchildren deciding, one by one, to also become followers of Jesus Christ.

Pictured in 1994, left to right, are Daniel, born in 1959; Harold, born in 1950; Kathy, born in 1955; Lynn, born in 1970; Joy, born in 1961; Leonard, born in 1954; and Floyd, born in 1956.

Chapter 15
The Music Plays On

So QUICKLY, James and I have gone through forty-seven years of marriage—busy and full years of raising a family, doing the business of Bergey's Dairy Farm and serving the Lord through our local congregation and the larger Mennonite Church. Despite the sometimes daunting tasks, God's enabling power has never failed us. That, working together as a family, and the faithful service of fellow workers have helped us rise to the responsibilities of the moment. The formula has proven particularly useful in our farm operation.

Because we wanted our children to learn—as James and I had—the discipline of work and responsibility, we began assigning chores at a young age, washing dishes and polishing dress shoes on Saturday, among other tasks.

After James' brother Clyde's death in 1961, and brother Byard's decision not to pursue farming, father Titus had turned over most of the business to James. Since we processed milk and cream in our small bottling plant and ran several home delivery routes, along with crop farming, there was never a lack of things to do. Nevertheless, as the boys grew, James was concerned that enough work existed around the farm for those who chose to continue in the family enterprise. We increased our herd several times, even though one or another of the children would occasionally leave for school, church voluntary service, or another job. Meanwhile, we hired someone to fill in the empty spots. Then, in 1978, after much urging and encouragement from numerous persons, we ventured into new territory with our own ice cream and first retail store here at the farm.

Lynn, our youngest, was in school by then and I was excited in this new undertaking. While I always tried to be in the house when Lynn returned from school mid-afternoon, James agreed soon that I should look after the store's day-to-day management. The job brought back memories of my working at Norfolk's old

City Market, and I thrived on the interaction with the customers.

By 1981, we were ready to expand our retail sales and opened our second retail outlet at Virginia Beach Farmer's Market. Six years later, May 1987, we moved into our third store on Battlefield Boulevard in Chesapeake. From 1987 through 1989, all of our children were working with us in the business.

Those, and the six years following, were as busy as any I ever encountered. I took care of inventory, ordering supplies, scheduling employees, and baking part time at the Battlefield store.

In 1965, Titus gave James and me full responsibility for the business.

Our family in 1970. In back, left to right, are Floyd, James Harold, Leonard, Kathy, and Daniel. In front are James, Joy, and myself holding Lynn.

Occasionally, when I was all but inundated with tasks I had assigned myself, James would chide, "Well, Mary, you have to be realistic."

Along with our business responsibilities, from 1984 to 1990, James and I were heavily involved with Deep Creek Mennonite—Mount Pleasant's nearby sister congregation—he as pastor and I as a member of the Sunday worship-music team. With the changes that had occurred in our local Mennonite congregations over several decades, musical instruments were no longer frowned upon, and I had taken up my guitar again, occasionally playing at home out of sheer enjoyment. My role at Deep Creek, however, forced me to brush up on skills dulled from years of disuse. The regular practice brought with it a greater appreciation than ever for the musical ability God had given me. With that, I vowed to use this gift for His praise and the furtherance of His kingdom.

When our time of service at Deep Creek ended in 1990, we returned to Mount Pleasant Mennonite. There, I soon became involved playing and singing with the children's Sunday school assembly. Enjoyable as that experience was, I could not have foreseen what more opportunities the Lord had in store for James and me.

* * * *

Growing older, most of us look forward to retirement and life at a more leisurely pace. However, when one's working years have followed a particular routine, the prospect of switching gears can bring on feelings of uncertainty. As I turned sixty-two in 1990, family members began urging me, "Mom, you need to slow down."

Part of me agreed with that sentiment; however, on the other hand was an ingrained lifetime of seeing a full day's tasks completed. Letting go of what I considered essential responsibilities turned into a yearslong process. James and I sought counsel from a Christian business adviser, but even with Mr. Broussard's able advice, the transition did not come easily. By 1993, though, plans were in place for me to give up major duties with Bergey's Dairy stores. Daughter-in-law Elsa agreed to take on my management position. While I would continue part time, I looked forward to some intensive housecleaning that had been neglected for years, and there would be time to do things with the grandchildren—at least two of the girls were anxious to have guitar lessons.

James, while still two years from retirement age, was nevertheless turning over more of his day-to-day responsibilities to sons Leonard and Floyd. If things continued to come together, we might see a not-to-distant future of leisurely travel or several other pursuits favored by retired couples.

As I have noted earlier, through all our years of farming and business, James and I never lost our ardent interest in foreign missions. That unwavering zeal began to bear personal fruit in February 1993, when a group of businessmen led by Sam Scaggs from Cornerstone Ministries of Harrisonburg, Virginia, went to Albania to explore the possibilities for helping Albanian entrepreneurs establish their own businesses.

Albania, long noted as Europe's poorest country, had thrown off forty-six years of harsh Communist rule just three years earlier in 1990. The trip to Albania turned into a heartfelt experience for James. Seeing the country's enormous social and spiritual needs left him deeply burdened. In one of his phone calls home, he broke down and wept. "Mary, the needs here are just so great. Would you consider coming along back to Albania for a term of service?

The thrill of a new challenge and our merged thought patterns after forty-four years of marriage, I believe, gave me the confidence to immediately answer, "Yes, James, I'll come along"- how different from my "Oh, maybe," along a moonlit path so long ago, when he had asked me on this journey of a lifetime!

James came home and as 1993 wore on, we began plans to return to Albania the following year. Along with James' trip, we had received additional encouragement from Gessina Blauw and Fatmir Lacej, who spent a week as our houseguests in March. Gessina, a native of Holland, carried a long-held zeal for Albania's spiritual needs and had traveled in the country before Communism fell in 1991. Fatmir, a Christian attorney with the Albanian

Chamber of Commerce, would later transfer to the country's Ministry of Trade and Transportation.

Meanwhile, we were also negotiating with Volunteers for Overseas Cooperative Assistance (VOCA), an agribusiness group active in development projects around the world. VOCA offered us service opportunities in Uganda, Africa, Russia, or Macedonia. While we might have preferred Africa–since our son Leonard had served in Ghana, during the 1970s–we chose Macedonia, instead, for its proximity to Albania. Since VOCA was paying our travel expenses, we had inquired of them about going on to Albania, after our monthlong dairy assignment in Macedonia. VOCA kindly consented to our request, as James and I worked out details for the longer stay in Albania.

Fortunately, those preparations were eased by our longtime interest and James' dozen years as a member of the Virginia Mennonite Conference Missions Board. David Yoder, Missions' president, and Willard Eberly, administrator for overseas missions were personal friends, as was Sam Scaggs of Cornerstone Ministries. In fact, Sam and his wife, Beverly, were formerly members here at Mount Pleasant.

Before departure time arrived in February 1994, Willard Eberly suggested I consider taking along my guitar. Musical instruments were scarce in Albania, and Willard believed my music could be an important aid in teaching young people to lead in worship. "But don't expect them to sing four-part harmony," he said, smiling.

I didn't in the beginning, but by our third term in 1996, two fifteen-year-olds: Spartak and Denado, and I sang "Silent Night," in three-part harmony-a rare treat for our audience. Along with that, four of the Albanian young people were playing instruments together in church services.

Upon our arrival in the city of Lezhe in March 1994, we were immediately struck by Albania's contrasts. Scenes from the pastoral countryside were straight off a landscape artist's canvas; far removed from the frantic scramble that today marks so much of life in the

Mary and James in Albania, 1994.

United States. Large flocks of sheep, goats, and even turkeys, dotted the beautiful green hills. The animals were always carefully guarded, sometimes by small boys or a mother and her daughter. Old men in well-worn suit coats, and faces leathered by wind and time, worked in the fields with hand tools and horse-drawn equipment.

One of the most delightful sights was the open display of camaraderie among children and adults. Women and girls walking hand in hand, boys as well, is common practice and isn't given a second glance, as it might be here in the United States. James and I promptly learned this natural friendliness extended even to us foreigners. After decades of being shut off from the outside world, the average citizen seemed extremely eager for knowledge about people and places beyond the nation's borders; in most instances, visiting in an Albanian home became a memorable experience.

Though small and crowded, the homes as a rule were spotlessly clean. Removing our shoes upon entering the home, we were warmly greeted with hugs and a kiss on each cheek. Once seated, the hosts would bring candy or some other sweet treat, along with espresso or Turkish coffee. Often, there was fresh fruit offered, as well. This custom of plying visitors with food and drink is so strong, that a family member will rush out to a nearby shop to buy refreshments, should the house be without when guests drop in.

Casual guests do not overstay their welcome–fifteen to twenty minutes at most. During that time, the conversation remains light, but attentive to the visitors. "Are you tired? What have you been doing today?" Departing, we were always urged, "Yes, you must come back again."

Few Albanian households have the conveniences we Americans take for granted, including refrigerators, ranges, washers, and dryers; however, one of the most difficult adjustments for us was the lack of heat in our apartment. Other than an electric hot plate for cooking, tenants usually get by without additional heat. Local people survive the winter cold by wearing thick layers of clothing. But being soft Americans, James and I, could not. We bought wood during our first term, and a propane gas burner the last two years. When neighbors dropped in, we always turned down the heat in response to their complaints. "Oh, we are too warm. It's too hot in here."

While the lack of modern appliances in Albania called up childhood memories of kerosene lamps and washboards, an early morning drive across the lowlands west of Lezhe, turned into far more than a leisurely country drive. The unpaved roads, the large drainage canals and banks overgrown with reeds were all so familiar. There was only one thing missing; and though unaware, I must have been listening, nevertheless.

At first sound, I knew it couldn't be what I seemed to be hearing. My imagination was playing tricks, or the car engine had taken on a strange high-pitched whine. Then, suddenly, there was no doubt, and I all but shouted, "Stop! James, stop! Hear them? It's frogs."

James braked and shut off the engine, as the air around us reverberated with thousands of frog voices. Like a giant wave the full-throated chorus swept away the years. Once again, I was a little Amish girl back at Moyock, North Carolina. There was our farm off Puddin' Ridge, with Dad, Mom, sisters, and brothers; and I, in childish innocence, trusting in the warm security of home and family. On a summer's eve, we children ran with cousins, Ilo and Marietta, calling and laughing across the lawn, while the grownups sat on the front porch and talked. A light breeze carried the wild honeysuckle's sweet perfume, as the surrounding twilight pulsed with the music of an invisible orchestra. Although no single tone prevailed over another, from high-pitched trills to deep bass croaks, together, the blended sound poured forth nature's symphony.

In a brief moment, I was back to the present, our vehicle stopped along a country road, with James and me listening to spring frogs–a rather ordinary exercise. Yet, for some unfathomable reason, sixty years and thousands of miles were bridged in an instant by something hidden deep in my soul. Why had the clamorous refrain left such an impression during my childhood? Did God have an underlying message there for me? I would need time to reflect, and later talk about it, before the pieces would begin to fit.

After two more yearlong terms, 1995–96, of church-planting in Albania, I have come to some understanding of what I believe God has been trying to teach me.

Beginning with the frogs: unattractive creatures though they are, frogs go about doing the things for which they were created, and making themselves heard is surely a primary behavior. Nevertheless, one frog alone, or even several together, brings on a mere sequence of sounds. It takes a chorus in full voice to transcend time and space. Whether a child of the 1930s, on a remote farm along the edge of North Carolina's Dismal Swamp, or a grandmother in 1994, on a morning drive along the Adriatic seashore, to my ears those froggy multitudes produced a special rendition of praise to the Creator.

Upon further consideration, I realize the significant role music has had throughout my life. Early on, I found special joy in Mom's singing as she went about her daily work. Later came the thrilling four-part harmony in our living room, when the Amish young people joined my sisters to sing and play their guitars. By early teen-age, I also took up the instrument; and though I put the guitar aside for a length of time to comply with church rules, I never gave up singing. As a trio, Leona Miller, sister Fannie, and I sang at Literary, weddings, and other church events.

After Fannie married and left the community, Maxine Warfel, Martha Hochstetler, Verna Mae. Orpha, Leona–Millers all–and I sang in a sextet together. Now in later years, God has used my guitar to bless many others. The experience has been altogether inspirational and humbling. In children's Sunday school, worship and praise services, and small family groups here at home and in Albania, the joyful responses remind me that music is a universal language, not contained by national boundaries.

For whatever has been said to this point, I want to now bring what I see as God's purpose for my life. Outside of His will, we are all unlovely creatures. Our own best efforts often produce little more than a lifetime of discordant croaking. Because they are sounds of our earthly existence, even the pleasant tones from a frog myriad, or a singing lady with a guitar, are but minute echoes of what God truly desires from His children.

It is when we allow Him to tune and shape us through the hardships and joyful events of our lives, that He exchanges our ugliness for His beauty. Through the love of Jesus Christ and by the power of the Holy Spirit, we become the Heavenly Father's voices and instruments, playing our roles in service to family, the church and community nearby, and to the far reaches of the earth, as well. Finally, when you and I have completed our last performance here, the Master Conductor will call us to Himself, as members of His own great Eternal Symphony.

The End

Index

Beard, Dena (Troyer), 109, 119. See also Troyer, Dena (Miller)
Beard, Sheldon, 54
Beard, Vernon, 44, 47, 51, 56
Bender, Herman, 100
Bender, Verna (Kemp), 100
Bergey, Amanda (Hendricks), 101
Bergey, April, 127
Bergey, Byard, 96, 116, 117, 129
Bergey, Clayton, 58, 97, 101, 105
Bergey, Clyde, 96, 97, 98, 116, 117, 118, 129
Bergey, Daniel, 115, 126, 127, 130
Bergey, David, 126
Bergey, Debbie, 126
Bergey, Dorcas, 127
Bergey, Elsa, 126
Bergey, Erin, 126
Bergey, Floyd, 115, 126, 127, 130
Bergey, Helen (Dickerson), 115, 117
Bergey, James "Harold," II, 107, 110, 117, 126, 127, 130
Bergey, James Harold "Jamie," III, 126
Bergey, James, 1, 84, 85, 98, 117, 130, 134
Bergey, Jennifer, 127
Bergey, Jesse, 126
Bergey, Joel, 126
Bergey, John David, 109, 110, 111, 112, 113, 114
Bergey, Katie, 126
Bergey, Laura Joy, 126
Bergey, Leonard, 115, 117, 126, 127, 130, 133
Bergey, Lori, 127
Bergey, Lynn, 115, 121, 127, 129, 130
Bergey, Mary (Troyer), 1, 6, 17, 23, 25, 30, 32, 44, 47, 84, 86, 98, 117, 130, 134
Bergey, Naomi (Kemp), 58, 89, 93, 101, 105, 117, 119
Bergey, Philip, 126
Bergey, Rachel, 127
Bergey, Ray, 117
Bergey, Rose, 126
Bergey, Sara Joy, 126
Bergey, Titus, 93, 105, 117, 129
Blauw, Gessina, 132
Brackbill, Milton, 81
Brunk, Sammy, 59
Buckwalter, Roberta, 109, 113
Buckwalter, Shirley, 109
Byler, Clarence, 82

Clendenning, Harold, 67
Conrad, Cleta, 100
Conrad, Dennis, 100
Conrad, Shad, 100
Cooper, Donna Faye, 25

Dickerson, Donnie, 117
Dickerson, Roy, Jr., 118
Dickerson, Roy, Sr., 117, 118
Dickerson, Sylvia, 117
Dickerson, Walter "Doc," 117, 118

Eberly, Willard, 133

Felton, Bruce, 47
Felton, Mamie, 35, 47

Harrington, Dr., 108, 114, 121
Hobbs, Nancy, 106
Hobbs, Ray, 106
Hochstetler, Carson, 59
Hochstetler, Emery, 55
Hochstetler, Martha, 109
Hochstetler, Milan, 59
Horst, Leah, 85
Horst, Mahlon, 85

Jantzi, Andrew, 71

Kauffman, Nelson, 83
Kemp, Malinda, 58, 97, 105, 117
Kramer, Eli, 26

Lacej, Fatmir, 132
Landis, John, 100
Landis, Mildred, 100
Layman, Amos, 84
Lehman, G. Irvin, 81
Lehman, Lula, 108

McAmore, Marie, 25
Miller, Andy, 24
Miller, Barbara, 13
Miller, Edna (Troyer), 15, 23, 25, 27, 47, 50, 51, 61, 109, 119
Miller, Francis B., 47, 50, 60, 61, 68
Miller, Ilo, 24
Miller, Ivan, 59

Miller, John, 27
Miller, Jonas, 6, 25
Miller, Lena, 60
Miller, Leona, 59, 60, 61, 83
Miller, Lydia, 58, 59, 73
Miller, Malinda (Slaubaugh), 3, 15, 24, 57
Miller, Marietta, 24
Miller, Philip, 120
Miller, Roy, 50
Miller, Rudy, 14, 15, 16, 24
Miller, Verna Mae, 82, 120, 121
Morris, Joy (Bergey), 115, 127, 130

Overholt, Abner, 27
Overholt, Delilah, 27
Overholt, Joe, 26, 27
Overholt, John, 26, 27

Painter, Dr., 112
Powers, Riley, 28, 29

Risser, Isaac "Ike," 100
Risser, Mildred, 100

Scaggs, Beverly, 133
Scaggs, Sam, 132, 133
Schilders, Ed, 17
Selp, John, 17
Shaddinger, Laura, 97, 98
Silsley, Christa, 126
Silsley, Jae, 126
Silsley, Kathy (Bergey), 115, 117, 126, 127, 130
Silsley, Matthew, 126
Snead, Otis, 85, 87, 94

Stutzman, Dan, 41
Sullivan, Eddie, 25
Sullivan, Esther, 25
Sullivan, Harvey, 25

Teague, Fannie (Troyer), 15, 23, 25, 29, 49, 50, 52, 97
Teague, Norman, 97
Tennefoss, Dorothy, 59
Tennefoss, Mabel, 59
Tennefoss, Thomas, Jr., 59
Tennefoss, Thomas, Sr., 59
Tice, Elsa, 82, 83
Tice, Evelyn, 82, 83
Tice, Naomi, 82, 83
Tice, Simon, 82
Troyer, Alvin, 15, 25, 27, 29
Troyer, Atlee "Bud," 6, 25, 31, 32
Troyer, Dena (Miller), 14, 18, 35, 42, 47, 52. See also Beard, Dena (Troyer)
Troyer, John S., 13, 14, 17, 119
Troyer, Lizzie, 23, 25, 27
Troyer, Malinda, 15, 22, 25, 27, 34, 50
Troyer, Simon, 13, 16

Warfel, Maxine, 97, 101, 109
Warfel, Rebecca, 84
Warfel, Stanley, 97, 101
Weaver, Ernest, 65, 68
Weaver, Herman, 65, 68
Wenger, Amos D., 58, 83, 124
Wenger, Gordon, 84
Wenger, Homer, 66
Wenger, Rhoda, 124

Yoder, David, 133
Yoder, John B., 18